Conversations with Spirit

Conversations with Spirit

A Life of Encounters, of the other kind...

Gordon Arthur Smith
and
Jacqueline Towers

Zambezi Publishing

First published in the UK: 2003
by Zambezi Publishing
P.O. Box 221 Plymouth,
Devon PL2 2YJ (UK)
Fax: +44 (0)1752 367 300
email: info@zampub.com
www.zampub.com

British Library Cataloguing in Publication Data:
A catalogue record for this book
is available from the British Library

ISBN -9533478-8-5

Cover design: © 2003 Jan Budkowski
Photos: some © 2003 estate of the late
Gordon Arthur Smith
others © 2003 Sasha Fenton
135798642

Printed in the UK by Biddles Ltd

Dedication

This book is dedicated to the memory of my Grandmother, Jessica Large, for being the first person to introduce me to the wonders of the Spirit world, and to whom I am eternally grateful.

Foreword
by Sasha Fenton

Gordon Arthur Smith was born in Norfolk on the 3rd December, 1924. He was the eldest child in a respectable working family. Fate decreed that he would spend as much of his childhood with his grandmother as with his parents, and this circumstance was partially responsible for taking his life in a completely different direction to that of his younger brothers and sisters. A frightening experience at the age of sixteen led him to start questioning such things as spirits and clairvoyance. After this, he discovered that his grandmother was a medium and a tealeaf reader (a common way of creating a psychic link in those days). His grandmother explained many things about the spiritual world to him, and although he didn't immediately plunge into what later became his life's work, events gradually nudged him in that direction.

Losing his family and suffering a severe and life-threatening illness were the inciting incidents that forced the change in his life. The door to this actually opened several days after he came out of hospital, when a friend took him to a spiritual healer. Little by little, Gordon became involved in the Spiritualist movement, first as a healer then later as a medium and psychic. For many years he gave his time and talents for nothing, supplementing his earnings by means of his engineering "day" job. Later he took up professional work as a founder member and psychic consultant for the British Astrological and Psychic Society.

Gordon's book is a fascinating story of how an ordinary man came to lead an extraordinary life. He tells us of his discoveries and lets us share the stories of his many clients and his experiences of psychic circles, Spiritualist Churches and centres. Many of the stories are amusing, while others are just amazing. Gordon shows us the disbelief and opposition that he met along the way, especially in the past when there wasn't the easy acceptance of these things that there is now. He talks of people who started out by ridiculing his beliefs, but who later learned for themselves of the existence of the spiritual realm. In later years, Gordon taught others how to do what he did, and this book carries on that work in some of its explanatory and teaching sections.

Gordon saw nothing special about himself, and he considered that he just did what he had to do. He worked right up to the very end of his life, despite having had a couple of heart attacks and suffering badly from asthma, bronchitis and arthritis.

Naturally, the everyday world of his work as an engineer, family life, friendships, his wartime Navy service and much else are retold here. As with many psychics, tragedy and loss played a part in his life. However, this was balanced by his wonderful experiences of the spiritual realm, the many friendships that this work brought him; including the opportunity to travel and to become involved in the world of show business.

One thing that almost escaped Gordon was true love, partly due to a strange ineptitude in his dealings with women. It is clear now that this was caused by the feeling that his mother had rejected him early in life, and it led him to demand more patience and attention than the women that he chose to attach to were able to give. However, right at the end of his life, he finally found what he had been longing for. He had almost two years of the purest and most selfless form of love in the shape of his dear friend, Jackie, who talked with him every day on the phone and helped him write this book. She will miss him more than words can say.

At the end of his life, Gordon's only regret was losing touch with his children all those years ago. He would have done anything to keep in contact with them, but in those days it was not possible. If you know anything about Gordon's son Philip and his twin daughters Karen and Andrea, please put them in touch with me and I will pass any messages on to his brother, Jeff, and make them aware of the existence of this book. I would love to hear of the surprise they would experience upon discovering what a fascinating and well-respected man their father turned out to be.

*****

I joined the British Astrological and Psychic Society in 1982, but it was only once I joined the committee that I got to know Gordon well. We both lived in Surrey, while the meetings were held in various parts of London and Gordon ferried me across London for some of our more distant meetings. We shared stands at festivals and travelled around the country doing psychic work. He also contributed a chapter to an earlier book of mine that had taken information from a number of psychic specialists. I was one of many people that Gordon worked and travelled with and one of the many who knew his kindness and gentleness. At different times he gave healing to my mother-in-law, my daughter and me and he never asked for anything in return.

I finished editing this book and sent the manuscript to Gordon to check through, but he was too ill to make the effort, so I told him to put it aside until he felt better; then, three days later Gordon Smith had passed away. It seems that he had kept going just long enough to finish his book. It was then up to his friend and amanuensis, Jackie Towers, to check the proofs, for me to finish the editing and put this book out into the world for him.

It was a pleasure to work on Gordon's book, and also a revelation. Knowing someone well is one thing, but this book gave me a precious opportunity to look into the large and generous heart of a truly good spirit.

Gordon Arthur Smith died at 9.30 a.m. on the 2nd July, 2002 in Basildon hospital in Essex.

One of a Kind
Foreword by
Jacqueline Towers

I first met Gordon at the twelfth annual Psychic Seminar, which was held in Bournemouth on the south coast of England in October 2000. I had been invited to attend by a mutual friend called Astrid Hansen, who Gordon had known for many years.

My attendance at this Seminar was a turning point for me - and this was solely down to Gordon. Although I had been reading the Tarot for many years, I did not practice it professionally, but I had now reached a stage in my life where I was seeking more involvement in psychic work. I had already been given too much proof of the existence of Spirit for me to be able to ignore it, so I very much wanted to work with it in some way. I went along to the Seminar in the hope of gaining inspiration as to which direction I should take. I had attended one workshop on the first day, but this had left me with many unanswered questions. I joined the other participants in the lounge and noticed a gentleman who was quietly sitting and smoking a pipe. So many people stopped to exchange a few words with him that I could see that he was "important", but he also appeared to be approachable. I took my courage into my hands, walked up to him and then asked if he minded answering some questions for me. He asked me what it was that I wanted to know, and I then proceeded to bombard him with questions - and I continued to do so throughout the Seminar. He kept telling me that I had the ability to work with Spirit and he asked me why I wasn't already doing so, then answering his own question by telling me that this was only because I lacked confidence. This was true, but it surprised me that he recognised it so quickly. By the end of the week, Gordon had given me enough encouragement for me to try my hand at mediumship and psychometry. These were things that I never thought I could be capable of doing, and something that I would never have attempted without Gordon's support. We spent many hours just talking - with me doing most of the talking, while Gordon, as always, quietly listened. From our conversations, I gleaned that he secretly wanted to write a book. I now know that I was spiritually guided to encourage him in this, because I persuaded him to dictate what he wanted to say on tape so that I could type it up for him. It was this that led to my unique friendship with him.

To me, Gordon Smith was an extremely special man - a "one of a kind" person. He was my mentor and he became a very special and totally irreplaceable friend. He gave me support, encouragement, confidence. He believed in me, not only as a person but also in the context of the work that I wanted to do, and he did everything and anything he could to help me develop. I found him to be a very kind and generous man who also had an impish sense of humour. He was often in great pain but he never complained. He was also a very modest and unpretentious man. He often used to say to me, "I'm no-one special, I just do what I do." That was so typical of Gordon. There is information that he imparted to me that has not reached this book, because it would have made Gordon sound boastful - which he most definitely was not. I feel extremely privileged and honoured to have been given the opportunity to know him in the way that I did, even if it was for a relatively short period of time.

We spent hours and hours on the phone, when he would supply answers to everything that I asked him - he always had the right answer. He was there to teach and advise me. He encouraged me to join the British Astrological and Psychic Society, and he was delighted when I passed my vetting and became a Consultant for the Society. The words that will remain with me are, "You can do it!" To each and every small achievement that I made, he would comment, "Good." These were simple words that meant so much, coming as they did, from him. Gordon always liked to keep things simple and easy to understand, and that was one of the things that made him unique. He gave so much of himself to others - not just his time, but also his wealth of knowledge that had been gained over the years. There must be thousands of people who Gordon has helped or healed and he has never asked for or expected anything in return. As a dear friend of mine said to me, "With him goes an encyclopaedia of knowledge that all those who were lucky enough to have known him can now no longer access."

I know that Gordon is happy to be "home" now, and to be surrounded by his family and friends. I also know that Gordon will never cease working - and neither will I, because I want him to be proud of me. During his last few hours with us, I had passed a message to him via his brother, Jeff, saying that he could not leave yet as he still had more work to do - and another book to write. Gordon said to his brother, "Tell Jackie and the others that I can still do my work, but now I will be able to do it without being interrupted!"

Gordon's activity was ceaseless. He travelled far and wide, both here and abroad. There are too many friends to mention who held him in high regard and who had great respect for the work that he did. He will be greatly missed by us all, but I think that we must all remember that he has only gone home, and that we will meet up with him again in our own time one day. He will continue his work - of that, I've no doubt.

So, my dear friend, let me take this opportunity to thank you so very much for allowing me into your life through this book, for the knowledge that you imparted along the way, for the laughter that we shared - and for introducing me to working with Spirit.

In my heart always until we meet again,

Your dear friend and grateful student,

Jackie Towers

June 2002

London

CONTENTS

CHAPTER ONE

Feelings of rejection

I had not always lived with my parents. Indeed, I had spent the first two-and-a-half years of my life with my grandmother. It was many years before I discovered the reason for this, but it appeared that my birth had been a difficult one. This was partly because I had been an 11 pound 8 ounce baby, but also because my mother contracted a kidney problem after the birth. Doctors were not as knowledgeable as they are today, so it had taken time for her to regain her health.

It was only when I was fifteen years of age and chatting with my grandmother one day, that I mentioned that I had always felt that my parents didn't want me. I then asked her why I had been so rejected at birth. She told me the reason and said that she had always thought that my mother would tell me what had happened. Throughout my childhood, my mother eased her family and health pressures by packing me off on a train by myself to stay with my grandmother for the longer school holidays and even for Christmas. This kind of practical solution to family problems was not uncommon in those days, but it left me with the feeling that my parents didn't want me. Until I really began to understand the ways of spirit, this fact influenced much of my later opinions and behaviour in detrimental ways.

It was 1928 and I was four years old. It was a nice day outside and I was wandering around somewhat confused. My mother was sitting on a chair outside the house, watching two men in brown coats who were busily taking the furniture out of it. The house was a two up and two down cottage arrangement with a shed at the bottom of the garden that also served as the loo that my mother frequently visited, because she was pregnant. I was watching the men load the furniture onto the two wagons and I was very intrigued by one of the wagons, which was a steam wagon of the kind that nowadays we would call a flatbed lorry. It was only a small construction, equivalent to a fifteen-hundredweight truck that we have today, but it was steam-operated and it fascinated me. The men were putting most of the furniture onto the steam-operated truck. I loved the steam wagon and I kept walking around it and listening to the "puffing" of the relief valve. All my mother would tell me was that we were moving so that we had more room, which we would need when my new baby brother or sister came along. I couldn't see the point, as to my mind, we had been quite happy where we were, but another baby was coming, and as our house was so small, my father had applied for more suitable accommodation.

We had been allocated a house in a village called Great Ryburgh, three miles outside of Fakenham, which was the town that we were leaving. Even at this age, I used to walk to the shops, as they were only a few hundred yards away. I sometimes shopped for the neighbours, in particular a blind lady who lived next door to us. Her husband was sighted, but she was getting on in years and if she needed something, she would knock on our wall to catch our attention. Sometimes she needed help, but most often she would ask if I could pop out to the shops for her. I took a little purse and a note to give to the shopkeepers. They would put the change in the purse and give me a brown paper bag containing the goods and the note.

I asked my mother where my father was and she told me that he was at work and could not come, so it was just a case of watching everything being put onto the trucks. Eventually everything was loaded. The chair that mother had been sitting on was put onto the truck, and my mother walked back into the house and asked me to go upstairs to make sure that nothing had been left behind. I came downstairs again, noticing how hollow the house sounded, with my footsteps echoing back to me as I trotted down the stairs. The only floor covering had been linoleum, with small rugs around the beds or at the top of the landing. I went outside and my mother climbed into the petrol lorry with the driver, but to my delight, I was told to ride in the steam lorry, so off we chugged. We did not have far to go.

We arrived at the new house, which turned out to be a semi-detached three bed-roomed house standing at the end of the road. It was in a group of eight properties, made up of four blocks of two. The house faced the main road into the town. What made it so wonderful for me was the long back garden, where there was plenty of room to run and play, and there was a front garden that was also large enough to play in. I ran out to the back garden and explored it while the men brought in the furniture round the pathway into the house. The linoleum came in first, but unfortunately it did not fit and my mother realised that sooner or later she would have to buy some more. The men then transferred all our remaining possessions from the wagons into the house.

The first thing to be done was to make a cup of tea, so it was straight into the kitchen where mother made a cup of tea for herself and for the workmen in gratitude for all their hard work. Our first house did not have a cooker, so everything had to be done on a coal-fired range, which meant that it had not been easy to make a cup of tea there, but now we had a cooker. Best of all was having a loo just outside the back door. We also had a "bathroom". This was a covered bath that was actually in the kitchen. There was a big board over the bath, and we would sit on this while eating our meals. When we wanted a bath, we took the top off, stood it against the wall and filled the bath with water.

When we arrived at the house in the village of Great Ryburgh, I was still fascinated by the steam wagon. I had often seen these vehicles driving around the town and carrying their loads, but I had not been so close to one before. So I went straight back out to the road where the steam wagon was still parked, walked around it, looking at it and listening to the little rattles and watching the movement of the valves. All too soon, it was time for the men to move on and I had to go back inside to help my mother. Not long after we arrived, my father came home.

My dad was a mechanic cum auto-electrician and he worked for a big garage in Fakenham. During the First World War, Dad had been in the RNAS (Royal Navy Air Service), and had worked as an engineer on aircraft components. The garage he worked at also dealt in aircraft components along with some bodywork, so my father was able to cash in on his aircraft knowledge.

Soon after arriving at the new house, I went outside, where I discovered a field on the other side of the road, opposite our row of houses. There was only one house on the other side of the road. We were right at the end of the village – at the "top end" as it was called. I could see our new neighbours going into our house to introduce themselves to my parents, and they brought items of food in with them. In those days, this pleasant practice was a common way of welcoming newcomers.

Then I found a field with a large tree in it that I could climb. I was almost five, nearly of school age and I was due to start school for the first time in the coming September, but for the moment my thoughts were only with this beautiful big oak tree. I decided I would climb the tree before going back indoors, and I thoroughly enjoyed doing so.

Several years ago, my nieces asked to see where I had been born and where I had lived when we moved to Norfolk, so I took them back to the village. Much to my delight, I discovered that the oak tree was still there. It must have some stories to tell, because it had been a large tree way back then in 1924.

We soon settled into our new home, and my father planted vegetables in the back garden and he also kept a few chickens in a run. As far as I recall, the field at the back of our garden grew wheat during the year we moved in. I used to go to the bottom of the garden and squeeze through the fence to watch the farmhands going around with their scythes in order cut a pathway around the edge of the field. This was to form a pathway for the tractor and the harvesting machine that was towed behind the tractor. The tractor had iron wheels and it was nothing like those of today. The harvester would reap the corn and a crowd of workers would follow, sheafing the corn by gathering it up in bunches and then standing these in "stooks" around the field to dry. A few weeks later, when the stooks were dry, the farmhands undid them, shook the heads into a sack and baled the remaining straw, which they then piled onto the end of a horse-drawn cart. The straw would then be taken back to the farm for winter feed or bedding. Wandering around these fields was a great adventure to me, as up to then I had only ever known a town situation. I had only ever gone out into the countryside with my father and mother for picnics on those weekends when Pop was able to borrow a car.

CHAPTER TWO

Schooldays

The time arrived when I was old enough to attend the village school. My mother took me to school on the first day, but after that I used to walk to school by myself, joining up with other children from the village on the way. The trip would start with two children from my end of the village. One of them was much older than I was, so he did not want to know me, but I used to chat to a small girl who was in-between my age and his. The children walked with me to the first farm, which was about a quarter of a mile down the road, where two more children joined us, one around my age and the other a little bit older. We continued on, collecting more children on the way. We all met in the village because the school was at the far end, along one straight road with little side roads going off to farms. The journey was a mile in total.

The schoolmaster and his wife were called Mr and Mrs Sapps. The schoolmaster was also the vicar of the village Church, and the Church was next door to the school. Mr and Mrs Sapps were the only two teachers in the village school and we stayed at the same school until we left at the age of fourteen. We were placed in various groups. I was put into the youngest group, which comprised ten or twelve children aged five to six years old. The second group went up to age twelve while the third group went up to the leaving age of fourteen years.

Mr and Mrs Sapps started each morning by giving us the work that they wanted us to do. As five-year olds, Mrs Sapps looked after us, because we were too young to be left without supervision. Every now and again she would check on the middle group before returning to us. Our classroom was actually just one large room with the three different age groups working in it. Surprisingly, it worked well, and I gradually moved up from group to group. I enjoyed going to school because the Sapps' made the work pleasant. To be sure, I had my ears "boxed" a few times and they occasionally smacked my behind. Later on my hands were caned a few times as well. I was no angel but I was not a particularly bad child and corporal punishment of this kind was common practice, so I didn't feel that I was being singled out.

*****

About the only thing that was at all out of the ordinary at that time related to the oak tree in the garden that I mentioned earlier. I used to go out, play around the tree, then go home, and tell my parents about the games I had played and whom I had played with. They knew that I was alone most of the time, but nothing was said about these non-existent "playmates". I now know that I was actually playing with "Spirit" children who I met in the tree and around the field. It all seemed perfectly natural to me and the "children" appeared normal. I later discovered that my mother understood what I was talking about - but my father definitely did not. When I used to recount the things I had done, he told me that I had a vivid imagination or that I was a liar. Well, there was not much I could do about it at the time, but from that time onwards, I vowed never to lie. Even at this young age I came to the conclusion that if people did not want to believe me, that was their problem.

*****

My sister Joyce was born in November 1929, and it was then that things changed slightly. My mother walked me to school and also occasionally collected me after school. If I was alone during the harvest or in the autumn sugar-beet season, I would often get a lift home on an empty cart. The railway station was only about a quarter of a mile away from the school, so the carts would take the sugar beet, beetroot, turnips and other vegetables to the station and load them onto the goods trains to be delivered elsewhere. They also used to bring down the bags of wheat, so the children used to hitch a lift back on the empty wagons. When I arrived home after such a journey, I used to get a bit of a tanning because I had dust or dirt on my clothes, but from what I recall it was never too bad. I think the smack or telling off was meant to teach me to keep my clothes clean, because in those days nobody had much in the way of spare clothes to change into, and washing was very hard work.

*****

When I was seven years old, I contracted St Vitus Dance and had to go into Norwich hospital for nine or ten months. It seemed like a lifetime. Owing to the lack of transport in those days, my parents could only visit at weekends when my father was able to borrow a car from the garage where he worked. The biggest "punishment" at that time came about because I was left-handed. I was told that this was "all wrong" and that I would have to change.

Note from Sasha: Like many psychics, Gordon has his moon in Pisces, and many people with the sun or moon in Pisces are either left handed or ambidextrous and some have very poor handwriting as a result. As it happens, Gordon's handwriting was actually very good until his arthritis made it hard for him to write. It is amazing how often this moon sign is associated with stress during childhood due to problems surrounding handwriting.

After a number of weeks I finally got out of bed, but I walked with difficulty, as I was still experiencing shaking around my joints. My left hand was tied to my side because I was being made to use my right hand - the people at the hospital told me that it was "unnatural" to use the left hand. Somehow I managed to cope and I slowly got better, and at last the time came when I was fit enough to leave the hospital. The shaking had gone and I was able to pick things up without dropping them. Fortunately, I had been given a certain amount of schooling while I was in the hospital to keep my schoolwork up to date.

I returned home and went back to school. I was given some extra work to do, including some homework so that I could catch up. My favourite subject was maths and Mrs Sapps made it a pleasure to learn, because she turned the times-tables into a song. I loved maths and English, I enjoyed school, and in fact, I enjoyed the village life as a whole.

One morning a little while ago I heard something on the radio that really made me laugh. The presenter was saying that a school had come up with a "new idea". Apparently, they were teaching the pupils to sing as part of a repetitive teaching method. I thought, "new" idea? That was what we practised in the 1930s!"

The Church used to put on festivities throughout the year for children as well as the adults, particularly at Easter when every child in the village was given an egg. The egg was hard-boiled and coloured, and each child's name was put on it. The eggs were then hidden in the Church or school grounds, at the back of which was an open area of bushes, trees and some grassland. It was lovely to go there at Easter to search for one's egg. If we did find anybody else's egg, we left it where it was because it had their name on it. The first child (never me) to find the egg was given a small chocolate egg as a prize. Those were enjoyable days. There was also a summer fair on the open grassland area, and much to my delight there were always steam traction engines to look at. The fascination that had begun during our house move when I was four years old has not left me, and I have loved them ever since. So much so, that if I am on holiday and if there is a steam railway or a steam show that is on anywhere, I always go along to see it.

My father loved to fish, indeed he was crazy about it, and he tried to teach me to fish but I never enjoyed it. I used to go to the river with my father; my six-year-old sister and my brother also used to come along. We would have a picnic while my father fished in the little river that ran along the bottom end of the village. I enjoyed the picnics but I just couldn't like the fishing. My father wasn't annoyed about my dislike because he was happy for me just to accompany him. When I knew I was going, I took a sketchpad with me and sat sketching the trees, bushes and fields. I am not particularly artistic but I enjoyed sketching at that time. I also loved to explore along the riverbank during the summertime, watching the crayfish in the water and seeing the dragonflies, butterflies and the birds.

Sometimes we would watch the wheat, oats and barley being harvested. It was great to go into the fields at harvest time because we used to get paid two or three old pennies to catch rats. As children, we used to chase and catch them and then put the rats into the little sacks that the farmer gave us, and he would pay us for each rat. The farmer would then take the sacks away. Much later in life, I heard that the farmer used to drown them in the water drums but we did not know that at the time. As far as we were concerned, the farmer just used to open the sacks and count the rats, and away we would happily go with our pennies. My father did not earn a lot of money, so I always gave half of what I received to my mother.

*****

We always had food on the table except for a short time when I was about nine years old. My father suffered from rheumatoid arthritis, and in those days the doctors couldn't alleviate it in the way that they can today. Father was sent away to the Droitwich Brine Baths for nearly nine months. My father had paid into what was then called the "Saturday Fund", which cost him two old pennies a week. This was like a Provident Society or something of that nature. While my father was ill, it paid out to my mother half a crown a week. (This was twelve and a half "P" in modern money, but the average worker's wage at that time was around £2 to £3 per week.) It was a small amount of money, but it provided us with the basics such as bread, butter, some cheese and so on. She was also able buy quite a few bananas, because oddly enough, in those days bananas were a cheap fruit. I frequently had an evening meal composed of banana sandwiches or ones made from lard that had been saved from the weekend meat meal.

Due to my father's engineering skills, before he fell ill, he had spent some time at the weekends at various farms in the area helping to fix broken machinery. While he was ill and away in hospital my sister, brother and I would look outside the back door to see if something had been left for us in the porch. On some mornings there would be a large sack of potatoes or vegetables such as carrots, cabbage, onions and so on. Local farmers who my father had helped left these provisions there for us. We never knew who left the food, and the only request that was made of us was that we fold the sacks back up after we had emptied them and leave them by the back door again. As if by magic, the empty sacks would disappear and new ones would take their place. Occasionally, we would find a piece of meat that had been put into the meat safe. This was like a wire-meshed cupboard, fitted onto the wall in the porch-way outside the door. The meat safe kept the meat away from the heat in the kitchen that was generated by the range. It was due to the kindness of these local farmers that we did not starve during that difficult time.

When my father came out of hospital, the doctors advised him to move away from Norfolk because it is a damp area, which was not good for his arthritis. Norfolk, Lincolnshire and all around that area, up as far as the Humber are "fenlands" and the fens are a very damp area. My father began to look through the newspapers for somewhere else for us to live.

*****

One day a broken down car was towed into the garage where my father worked, and Pop stayed on late in order to repair it. The owner of the car spoke to my father and told him that he worked for a company in London and was travelling in the Norfolk area in connection with his job. My father mentioned to the man that he needed to move because of his health and that he was looking for work elsewhere. Not long afterwards, the man went back to London and then sent my father a letter with an invitation to attend an interview for a job at Park Royal in North West London. Father was accepted for the job and he soon found somewhere for us to live.

We packed our home up for the journey to London, where we were to live in a tiny house that my father had found for us. When my mother gave the removal men the address, they told her that that was not the address that they had been given. I remember this because there was an argument about it. They definitely had a different address, but this turned out to be a seven-roomed flat that, unbeknown to us, my father had managed to acquire. And so it was that in 1935 we moved to North West London. In the meantime, I was still going to my grandmother's house in Hunstanton for the holidays. I enjoyed my visits to Hunstanton, which is a seaside place, but the most interesting fact is that my grandmother sometimes made strange remarks to me about what I later learned to be spiritual matters.

CHAPTER THREE

A message from "the other side"

In September 1939 when the Second World War broke out,
I was fifteen years old and I had to leave school. This was partly
because I was now beyond the school leaving age, and partly
because the local government decided to use my school as an
auxiliary fire station, which meant that the children had to leave
or be split up. Some of the children were evacuated to Canada or
America. I went back to my grandmother's home in the town of
my birth, Hunstanton. The family was now becoming more
numerous and my mother was evacuated away from London. The
authorities said that I was too old to be an official evacuee, but
that I was too young to be left with alone with my father. He
remained in London because his job was considered to be war
work. Owing to his electrical expertise, my father had become an
Inspector for the Air Investigation Department. If an aircraft
crashed (British or foreign), he would go along with a team of
men and they would salvage what they could so that the parts
could be used again.

It was toward the end of my stay in Hunstanton that my
grandmother commented that I would be pleased to get back to
London. It was at this point that I said that I wasn't particularly
bothered about being with my parents, as I had never felt wanted
by them. It was then that the conversation about my first two or
three years took place. Once this door to the past had been
opened, we talked for ages. My grandmother assured me that my
mother did love me, but that she was also aware of the fact that
my grandmother had become very attached to me during that first

two-and-a-half year period, hence the time I periodically spent
with her over the years.

*****

I found a morning job delivering bread. My grandfather
worked as a professional gardener for the local Council. He used
to tend the Memorial Gardens at the top of the cliff, which were
also the pleasure gardens, in preparation for the visitors who came
throughout the summer months. Hunstanton is a holiday resort,
and in those days there were bus excursions and trains that
brought day-trippers and holidaymakers throughout the summer
months. It was grandfather's job to keep the gardens, flowers and
the decorations tidy and he made a good job of it. In addition to
this day job, his wartime duty was that of an ARP (Air Raid
Patrol) Warden. This entailed him having to go out at night and
look for war damage, because enemy aircraft flew over that part
of the coast. The enemy aircraft flew over us on their way to
Birmingham, Coventry or other similar towns and cities and
occasionally they would drop a few bombs over Hunstanton on
their way there or back. My grandparents lived close to the gas
works, so this made them a particular target. My grandfather was
always worried in case the Nazis decided to drop a few bombs on
the gasworks during the night, because we would be in danger
and he would not be there to help. He gave us strict instructions
that if the sirens sounded when he was on duty at night, we were
to take our lanterns and our books and go into the wash house,
which was a windowless brick building in the back yard.

My uncle was a cinematographer operator at the local
cinema, so he didn't come home from work much before eleven
thirty in the evening. He worked two days a week on the
afternoon matinees, but otherwise he did not go out much before
half past four to five in the afternoon in order to prepare
everything for the evening cinema programmes.

One night, at around one thirty in the morning the sirens
sounded. I got up quickly and started to dress. I was only half-
dressed when for some reason I looked up at the window and saw

the reflection of a woman from the waist up. She looked straight at me and I could see her head and mouth moving. This frightened me enough, but then she spoke to me, saying that I should go back to bed. "You will be all right".

I was in a state of absolute terror, so I ran into my grandmother's room, only for her to tell me off because she was only half-dressed! When she saw the expression on my face, she asked me what was wrong. She asked me to describe the woman that I had seen. She then told me to go back to bed. I protested but she repeated that I should return to bed and I duly did so.

I got up as usual at six the next morning in good time for my deliveries, the first of which were to the local hotels around the town. After this I would return home to pick up the loaves that I had parked there for the later household deliveries. When I came in, I tackled my grandmother about the events of the previous evening, but she told me that she would explain everything when I returned home from work. It was not wise to argue with my grandmother, so I went back to work. When I arrived back home at midday, my uncle was there and my lunch was already on the table. My grandmother signalled to me to keep quiet until it was time for my uncle to leave for his matinee performance. Eventually I got the opportunity to ask my grandmother to explain what the previous evening had all been about. My grandmother asked me once again to describe the lady I had seen - this time in more detail - and also to repeat the exact words she had used. I did so and she smiled with a conspiratorial air, saying that it was now time for me to know.

"Know what?" I asked.

Grandmother told me that the lady who I had seen was my mother's sister, Lottie, who had died some months before I was born. Apparently, she had been a seamstress in the Royal residence at Sandringham, and in those days, the pins that they used to pin up the fabrics with were iron-based. It seems that she had put two pins in her mouth and something happened that caused her to swallow them. One passed through her, but it transpired that the other pin had gone through her stomach lining, when it became lodged in her liver where it rusted and poisoned her.

My grandmother then spent the next couple of hours telling me what "Spirit" was. She told me that she had full knowledge of it, along with an acceptance of the Spirit world. She also told me where we all go once this life is finished. She explained how and why it worked. She reminded me how, when I had been younger, sometimes people had knocked on the door and that she had told me to go out and play and not come back until I was called.

Grandmother explained to me that people used to come and see her for help and guidance. She told me that the first thing she would do was to make a cup of tea and chat to the person, then she would read the tealeaves that remained in the cup. She explained to me that she would start by swirling the cup around and then gently turning it upside down to get rid of any liquid. She would then look at the cup and watch the tea leaves taking on a pattern. She would call on her "friends" to ask them what the pattern meant. She asked her "friends" why the person had come to her. When she received a response, she would go on to say what she felt needed to be said. She moved on to explain that these "friends" to whom she referred were friends in "Spirit", like the aunt who had appeared to me as a vision in the window. She told me that only the body dies, but that we - as "Spirit" - move on to a different world. She then said that we took our personalities across with us and carried on working. She told me that we retained our character, our likes and dislikes (at least to begin with) as we started our journey on "the other side". Grandmother said that "Spirit" was there to help us at all times. She said that we should remember that this was not something to be kept in a box.

Back in the 1930s and 1940s, these things were not spoken about openly, but my grandmother told me that for some people, this became a part of one's life. She explained that I had inherited this gift from my mother and she told me that this was why my mother always knew whether I was telling the whole truth about something or not.

Gordon's comments

Grandmother claimed that the spirit world had become part of her world, and looking back, I can see that it had always been part of mine too. As you will see, I came through some hair-raising times during the war. I have since looked back and recalled the many times when there was no logical reason for my survival.

At the time of this first conversation, I accepted the things my grandmother told me. Once I began to investigate these things for myself, I discovered that things were just as my grandmother had said. The essence of which was:

"Spirit is there. He, it, they, are part of you and should always be part of you and not kept in a separate compartment."

When looking back, I can see how Spirit has looked after me. For example, I remember one occasion when we were under attack by the Japanese. I was the Number Four gunner, which meant that I fed the ammunition to the gun crew. Our gun took a direct hit and when the smoke cleared I could see that the gun was all twisted. My three colleagues were all lying injured on the deck, but all I had was a torn uniform - and not a mark on me.

When I was in the Fleet Air Arm, I was occasionally allowed to take flying instructions on my days off. On one occasion, the training aircraft had just been overhauled and I was asked to go along with another pilot and take it for a test flight. We reached five hundred feet, the engine seized up and we nose dived back down towards the jungle. The sudden movement knocked me unconscious and the aircraft crashed into the trees, breaking up in the process. When I was rescued, all I had was a bruise on my forehead, a cut on my wrist and another on my back. My colleague should have received fewer injuries than I had, because he had been sitting behind me, but he had a broken collarbone, a broken leg and several other injuries. Once again, I had been protected.

It is only at those times that I began to understand what my grandmother had been telling me all those years ago. I did not understand it completely until later on when I did my own investigations into the subject. It was really only then that everything that she had said to me during those early conversations became truly clear to me.

One has to bear in mind that all this had taken place during the 1930s when such things were not discussed, and when it all took place behind closed doors. My grandmother said that her sister - and my great aunt, Hilda, who lived nearby, also believed in "Spirit". Grandmother said she would arrange for me to go and talk with great-aunt Hilda so that she could also tell me what she knew, because it was now clear that I should understand these things. On that first occasion, Grandmother and I spent the whole afternoon discussing the subject, but it still left me with a lot of unanswered questions in my head. A few days later, I went to see my great-aunt Hilda, and what she told me in her own way boiled down to much the same thing - in short, that it was all about "Spirit". This was just as well, because at that point in my life I was becoming increasingly aware of "Spirit", myself and if nobody had given me any kind of explanation, I would have wondered if I was right in the head or not.

CHAPTER FOUR

Work and the Armed Services

Before I left school, I had planned on going into accountancy owing to my talent for mathematics and my love of the subject. By the time I left school, I had gained a Royal Society of Arts Certificate in maths, which was considered to be very good. The modern equivalent might be one of those AS levels, somewhere between a GCSE and an "A" level. On the basis of that result I went to work into an accountant's office, on the understanding that I would receive training as an apprentice. I was supposed to have one day's instruction per week, with more training as my knowledge grew. In the event, I spent six weeks sweeping the floor, picking up rubbish, making tea and doing other menial tasks and at no time was I given any instruction whatsoever.

I went to my old Headmaster and told him about the situation and he said that I should ask my boss why I was not being taught anything useful. When I did so, the boss responded by telling me to go and make him a pot of tea. When I returned, I poured out a cup of tea and took it in to him, leaving him the pot - suitably covered - so that he could refresh his cup if he wished. He said he would call me back in to explain. About an hour later, he started swearing and calling for me. When I went in, he complained that the tea was cold and he promptly told me to make a fresh pot. I explained that I had made a fresh pot of tea but that it had been an hour ago. He retorted that it was not my place to argue with him because he was in charge and that he would teach me some manners. He then became extremely abusive, upon which I picked up the cup of tea and poured it over his head. Needless to say, that was the end of my career in that office!

When I was seventeen I was called back to London, as I was now no longer exempt from war work. My father arranged for me to become an apprentice at the factory where he worked, so it was here that I first began to learn about machinery and engineering. I had been working in the factory for approximately six months as an apprentice before the foreman told me that he expected to receive conscription papers for eight of the apprentices. He said that he had been told to let four of us go, but that he was not sure which four he wanted to let go. I told him that I would like to be one of those to be chosen, because my father's presence made me unpopular with the other apprentices. My father was head of a department and he used to come in every now and again with little jobs for me to do so that I could gain some experience of working on the various machines. I was doing more work than they were, but somehow they managed to work out that this added up to an advantage over them which they disliked. I explained this to the foreman and he understood.

He suggested that I go to the Recruitment Centre to volunteer for the Navy, because if I did not volunteer, I would be conscripted into the Army as an engineer and this would not be as advantageous. On his advice, I took myself off to the Recruitment Centre and volunteered for the Royal Navy.

Typical of the many muddles and changes that occurred to so many volunteers and conscripts at that time I was told to join the Royal Air Force, on the basis that I was already in the Boys Air Training Corp at the time. I went to the RAF station but I wasn't happy there. There wasn't much I could do about this, but six weeks later I received a bulky brown envelope with my father's handwriting on the outside. I opened it up to discover my call-up papers for the Royal Navy. It may have been a coincidence, but my belief is that Spirit had started to work on my behalf.

I went to the Adjutant at my RAF camp and asked him what I should do about the papers. He said that I should do nothing and that he would destroy them. Just as he said that, the Duty Officer walked in and asked, "Destroy what?" The Adjutant explained the situation and the Duty Officer told him that he could not do that. He commented that I had volunteered for the Royal Navy and that it was the senior service, so it took precedence - and anyway it was entirely my choice. That was how I left the RAF and joined the Navy.

On the day that I was due to travel to the Navy camp, I was given a set of overalls and a pair of plimsolls in exchange for my RAF uniform. It was a bitterly cold winter's day and I began the three-mile walk along the road carrying my belongings. I had just left the camp and started to walk, when seemingly out of the blue, a fifteen-hundredweight truck (about the size of a jeep) appeared beside me. The driver asked if I would like a lift and I gratefully accepted. It was nice and warm inside the truck. The driver asked me where I was going, while explaining to me that he was going to a nearby farm. He said he would drop me off about a quarter of a mile down the road from the Daedalus camp, because that was where he needed to turn off. When we reached the turning I got out and thanked the man profusely as he had been very kind to me during the journey. I continued to walk along the road to the camp, following the directions the driver had given me. The driver turned into the side road and disappeared - and I do mean disappeared! One minute the vehicle was there, while the next minute there was nothing to see. I thought no more of it and just assumed that he had driven off rather quickly. I continued along the road to the Navy Camp and reported in.

The Petty Officer asked me where I had come from and why I had not been transported. He told me that the RAF should have transported me, and I replied that all they had given me was what I had with me. The Petty Officer took me in to see the Officer of the Day to explain this to him. The officer asked me if the RAF had told me anything. I replied that all I had been told was to return the overalls and plimsolls to the RAF camp once I had been kitted out. While being kitted out I told the Petty Officer that, as it happened, I had not walked all the way as I had been given a lift.

He gave me a strange look and cocked his head on one side, then the other officer exclaimed, "Excuse me, but where did you say you the vehicle had turned?" I said it had turned off about a quarter of a mile back down the road. He then asked me to take him to the gate and show him. He looked puzzled and said, "That is the back way into this camp and it only goes on for five hundred yards, and we know the gate is locked and that nobody has asked for it to be opened!" I responded by saying that the driver had mentioned that he was on his way to visit a farm. The officer said that there had been farms in the area but that they could not be reached from that particular road. He said that I must have been mistaken and I agreed that perhaps I was - even though I knew I had not been. So, this time Spirit had been working with me in a manner worthy of the X Files.

*****

I started my basic training in Lancashire. The idea was that I would be trained as an accountant, but in true armed service style, I was put to work of a quite different kind. I was sent to Chatham to be a ship/shore electrician. Apparently there were no vacancies for accountants or "ships' writers", as they were called at the time. After a very concentrated six month training course on ship/shore electrics, I was shipped out to a transit camp. Naturally, I arrived to discover that there were no requirements for a ship/shore electrician, but I saw a notice on the wall announcing that aircraft electricians were needed for the Fleet Air Arm. I went to the Master at Arms and asked him if I would be eligible to apply for the post. He told me that he would look at my papers. When he came back, he confirmed that as a volunteer I was eligible, and that he would put me forward for it. He asked me if it was something I preferred to do but I said that there seemed to be little choice, as there didn't seem to be a suitable position for me anywhere else. I then went to Henlow in Bedfordshire and Melksham in Wiltshire to learn about the electrical systems on aircraft. After this, I was supposed to join a minesweeper as an electrician but then I was told to ignore that order and continue with my training. I later discovered that the minesweeper I was supposed to join had been sunk! Spirit was looking after me again! I finished my training and was sent to Scotland for exams and follow-on training at Dunfermline.

I was sent to Liverpool and then to America to pick up a "banana boat". The Navy used to convert lease/lend cargo ships that had large capacity and holds that could be used as hangers. Aircraft lifts were put into these ships so that they could be converted into mini aircraft carriers. Before the war, most of these ships really had been used for transporting bananas… hence their name. When we arrived, we discovered that the ship we were supposed to pick up was still only a hull. Very little work had been done on it and it would be a number of months before it could be ready for service, so we re-boarded the troop ship that we had arrived on and sailed back across the Atlantic!

Whilst we were crossing the Atlantic, two floating mines suddenly appeared. They were supposed to be tied down but according to the ship's crew, they had broken their moorings and were free-floating. The mooring consisted of a cable that was attached to either a heavy lump of iron or a piece of concrete or something similar that had been dropped into the sea. Under normal circumstances, this meant that the mine was under about six feet of water – just enough depth to catch the hull of an unsuspecting ship as it passed over it, but these mines were clearly visible.

Our ship happened to be a large troop carrier called the Oronty, so there were Army personnel aboard. They were ordered to shoot at the mines to try and blow them up so that they could no longer represent a danger to us or to any other ships that may pass. After a while, one of the men stopped for a break and I asked if I could have a go; my Officer-in-Charge who was nearby at the time, agreed that I could. I picked up the rifle, fired a shot and blew up one of the mines! Despite the fact mines are between four to five feet in diameter and ball-shaped, it is no good shooting randomly at them. Each one has a number of one-inch glass containers, about one inch in size, sticking out of them and it was these that detonated the mines when ships brushed over them. These detonators were made of glass that was covered with soft lead. The glass vials were filled with acid and when one of these was broken, the mine exploded. I knew that I was the one responsible for blowing up one of the mines, because I was the only one who was shooting at the time. When the second mine exploded there were three or four men firing at it, so nobody knew exactly who had hit it. Because I had been the one to blow up the mine, my officer recommended me for a Marksman's Badge - and this was wonderful, because it meant an extra three-pence a day on my pay!

The rest of our voyage across the Atlantic was trouble free and soon we were passing through the Straits of Gibraltar into the Mediterranean. Then we took the old Pacific and Orient route across the Mediterranean, down through the Suez Canal and on to Bombay where we were put ashore. Then we boarded a second ship and after three or four weeks at sea the officers found some work for us to do.

We were a NOTU Unit, which was a Naval Operational Training Unit. Pilots who had gained their wings England were sent to the Pacific, Indian Ocean and surrounding areas to train in Pacific conditions. If a pilot flies over the sea in northern latitudes such as Britain or North America, he can see the division between the sky and the sea. However, in hot areas such as around Australia, India and the Far East, the sea is a like a mirror and unless there are waves, it is hard to see where it starts and ends. The pilots had to learn how to rely on their instruments in order to know when they were close to sea level and our job was to maintain the aircraft they used for their training.

We were also keyed-up for "action stations", as we had some fighter pilots on board who would fly out to fight the Japanese if they came anywhere near us. We had been out at sea for seven or eight weeks when we experienced a kamikaze attack. Our ship was damaged and it needed to be towed back into port. We were transferred to work on an airstrip on Ceylon (now called Sri Lanka). We stayed there several months before going back to Trincamalee, the port where the ship had returned to be re-fitted and then setting off again for training at sea.

We had only been at sea for about seven or eight weeks when we were bombed again. I think the Japanese Intelligence knew what we were doing. On this occasion, we were more severely damaged than previously and our superiors told us that it would take a very long time to repair the ship again. We were towed back into Trincamalee and sent back to the emergency airstrip to do coastal work. In total, we were in Ceylon for nearly two years, and then at the end of 1943 we were transferred to India. In 1944, we were transported to a permanent airbase near Madras called Tambaram.

While I was in Asia, I enjoyed visiting any villages and native quarters that happened to be close by. If I found myself in the vicinity of a temple where there were monks to be found, the monks often asked me to visit their temple. The first time that this happened, I mentioned it to our Religious Officer. He looked thoughtful and commented that it was odd as I wasn't a Moslem and I didn't belong to any other unusual religion. I told him that I considered myself to be Church of England. The officer asked me why, under the circumstances, I thought this was happening. I replied that I hadn't the foggiest idea.

We were given some leave, and one of the officers organised a coach trip to Kandy. Kandy was not the capital of Ceylon but it was nearby and it was a Spiritual town, perhaps a little like a cathedral city in Britain in days gone by. Several religious sects and cultures had Temples in Kandy, and on this occasion we were to visit the Hindu "Temple of the Tooth". This temple was in the middle of a lake and could only be reached on foot via a catwalk that was suspended across the lake. We walked across the catwalk to the landing at the front of the Temple. There we saw two monks and the one in charge was chatting with my officer. There were forty of us in the group, and as we walked onto the landing at the front of the temple, the monks selected several men for a separate group and told them to stand to one side. I found myself in this separate group of six men. My officer told us that we had been selected to go into the Inner Temple, and he said that we should take off our boots and socks and leave them by the door. The officer stressed that only the six men chosen would be allowed into the Inner Temple while the rest would be shown around the Outer Temple. The six of us were ushered into the Inner Temple where we were given information about the faith, what the various statuettes and symbols meant and a general picture of what was taking place.

As we were leaving, the chief monk remarked that a couple of the men in our group seemed to understand (although I am afraid I did not at the time). He commented to the effect that we were to go away and "use our gifts and prosper". We rejoined the main group and looked around the Outer Temple before returning to the coach. The six men chosen were teased because we had been selected for special treatment, but I have to say that at that time, I didn't give the incident another thought. Twenty years had to pass before the significance of those words spoken by that monk in the Temple of the Tooth in Kandy meant anything to me.

Another experience happened in a little place called Annaradapura that was in the north of Ceylon. There, they had a beautiful statue of a Buddha. There were seats outside the Temple and I sat down to have a smoke on my pipe and to chat with some of the monks. Once again, I was invited into the Temple. While on this visit, I felt that I was unconsciously being shown that we can all live together. I really do wish this could happen around the world today.

I spent the last six months of the war in the south Pacific in South East Asia Command (SEAC), and I was moved to India just outside Madras. The Japanese were disrupting the shipping; so much of the work was being done from shore. We were posted to Tambaram where we set up a camp. I became a driver for the Navy. It may appear strange that all ships have their own drivers, but whenever we were in dock we had to pick up stores. The wagons were loaned to us, but the drivers had to be supplied by the ships themselves. When we had arrived at Tambaram, someone told me that my records showed that I hadn't had a proper driving test and that I would need to take one. When I think back now, I would love to see those convicted of dangerous driving today being made to take the Navy driving test. Believe me, they would find it quite daunting - it takes four hours!

My time overseas came to an end six months after the end of the Japanese war, during which time our Squadron was chosen to clear up the various bases around the area. There was lease/lend material such as aircraft, tools, supplies and a hundred and one other items to be packed up and returned to the Americans. We went around clearing these bases, transporting the material back to a shore base and then transferring it to a port where the American ships would come in to collect it.

On completion of this work, I was shipped off to a transit camp just outside Bombay, where I was told that I was to be shipped out to a troop ship the following day. The next morning, we discovered that everything was locked - the gates had been locked and barred and there were armed guards on them. We did not understand what was going on. A little later, almost three thousand men from the camp were gathered together and the officers told that we were being confined to camp under six weeks quarantine. Apparently a case of bubonic plague had been discovered! This plague is still prevalent in parts of the Far East. We filled in the time as best we could. One or two men even tried unsuccessfully to escape, but they were shot and they ended up in the sick bay. At long last, someone told me to pack my kit because

I was going home. I went down to the dockside, boarded the fast liner, Ile de France, and began my journey home back to the UK.

*****

On arrival in the UK, we disembarked at Southampton and were transported to Lee-On-Solent, which was to be my main base. They gave me six weeks leave and said that after this, they would make a decision as to whether my application for a permanent position with the Navy would be granted.

A couple of weeks into my leave my eyesight failed. The doctor told me that four years of living and working in brilliant light had affected my eyes, and that the fast trip back on the Ile De France hadn't given them time to adjust, so this had damaged my eyesight. I was sent to the Sterks Martin Clinic and slowly my eyesight began to return; it eventually became about ninety per cent of perfect, but I needed spectacles from then on. Once out of hospital, I returned to the transit camp at Lee-On-Solent. The clinic had kept the Navy informed of my condition throughout this period and I had received a special pension on top of my pay, but once back at Lee-On-Solent I was demobbed.

*****

I spent the next few weeks orientating myself and getting used to civilian life again. I managed to find a couple of small jobs but it took me just over a year to find permanent work. The men had started coming back from the European theatre of war over a year earlier, so most of the jobs had already been taken. Female workers had been welcomed into the world of work during the war, but they were now sent home in order to free up the work for the returning servicemen. The first of these small jobs actually involved me in more war work and the second ended when the governor decided to move away from the area. So, that was the end of an era and the end of the early part of my youth.

CHAPTER FIVE

Family... oh dear!

While I was in the Navy I discovered dancing! This was a great pastime, both while I was on board ship and on the shore base. *(Note from Sasha - moon in Pisces people are usually fond of dancing and often very good at it).* Once I was home I joined two dance clubs and had a partner in each. Both partners knew of each other and after a year (the end of 1947), I began to realise that both ladies thought that I would marry them. We didn't sleep with unmarried women friends in those days, so when a woman became interested in a man, she expected him to "get down on one knee"; I realised that I liked them both, so I decided to have a talk with my mother. My mother suggested that I take a three-month break from them both and that I should meet the one that I really missed on my birthday. I took my mother's advice and I finally got engaged to Joyce. Neither set of parents had much money after the war years, so while they helped out as much as they could, it was a case of getting much of what was needed together for a wedding by us.

Just before the wedding, I went to my doctor and asked for an examination, because while in Ceylon, I had had a tuberculosis scare. My doctor arranged for me to be examined in a hospital where he acted as Consultant one day each week. I told my fiancée about this and she asked if she could also have an examination, because she admitted to me then that she had had "women's problems". My doctor arranged for us to attend together. We both went to St Thomas' Hospital in London, and at four thirty in the afternoon I was given a clean bill of health. The mark that had appeared in the X-ray of my lung was an old pleurisy scar from childhood. Joyce was told that all was not well, but that we should get married and leave things as they were for three months. We were advised that if we were still worried, she would have to return to St. Thomas' for an operation. When we returned, the doctor laughed, because nature had sorted things out and my wife was pregnant! We went back home happy with the news, but now we had to consider our living accommodation, because we had taken it on condition that we had no children. We looked for a larger flat, but in the meantime Joyce and I went back to our respective parents for a while, partly in order to save money, now that we now had a baby on the way. A couple of months later, Roy found us an unfurnished flat and we gratefully moved in.

My wife had the baby and everything was going along smoothly - or so we thought. Soon after this, my father-in-law contracted cancer and within six weeks he had died, leaving my mother-in-law (an asthmatic invalid) living in rather a large flat on her own. My wife's sister was getting married, so she took our flat while we moved in with my mother-in-law in order to care for her. She spent most of the day in bed with various oxygen bottles around the bed.

My wife's youngest sister, Maureen, had a serious behavioural problem and she started to cause problems for us. I went to see the Probationary Service and she was put under their control. She had to pay weekly visits to her allocated Probation Officer to show that she was conducting herself properly. In the meantime, my mother-in-law was taken into University College Hospital in London for an operation on her chest to try and relieve her breathing, and this was pretty successful. My wife and I brought her home on the evening that Maureen was due to visit the Probation Officer. We arrived back at the flat as Maureen was just leaving. We had explained the situation to my mother-in-law, but when she saw Maureen and asked where she was going, she promptly told Maureen to stay put and said that she would sort things out herself. Needless to say, the problems started up again. The Probation Officer came to the flat and spoke to my mother-in-law. He tried to explain to her that Maureen had been behaving much better since she had dropped the crowd that she had been running around with, and that things were now getting resolved. My mother-in-law refused to accept this. The situation went from bad to worse, and that was the last thing we needed with our baby son, Philip, now in the middle of things.

I looked around for some other solution, but in the meantime a firm in Crawley took me on to build aircraft simulators for pilot training. I had to prove my commitment to this job by commuting for six months, after which I would be allocated a home. When we saw the pleasant new house in Crawley, Joyce took one look and walked straight out again saying, "Yes please!"

When we went back to the office to sign the papers, the lady in the office gave me a strange look and commented that she had not heard any complaint from us. I asked her why we should have complained, and she said, "The house number!" It was 13. I told her that she would not hear any complaint from me, so with that she said, "Sign here, the house is yours." So we moved to Crawley, and at last everything was going well. That was, until the firm made me redundant!

I was redundant for ten months, during which time I supplemented the meagre dole money by doing odd jobs. I went to the Labour Exchange every Tuesday to "sign on". After ten months, Mr Evans, the Supervisor, buttonholed me and said, "I've been waiting for you to come in, Gordon. Here's a railway warrant and a green card. You've got an appointment for an interview in Wandsworth for work at Gatwick Airport." I got the job and then reported to the TransAir office at Gatwick Airport after two weeks. I worked at Gatwick Airport for three years until 1960, and then Civil Aviation Authority decided that Service weren't good enough for us to continue working with civil aircraft. Luckily, I was designated for a job in the office until I found further employment.

I saw an advert in the newspaper for a Service Engineer and went along for the interview. It was one of the most stupid interviews I have ever had - yet it was a successful one. Six applicants had been selected to attend an interview at a hotel in Brighton for a company based in Halifax that wanted Southern Area Engineers. I was the final one of the six and a Mr Addy was my interviewer.

The first thing he said to me was "How far is the station from here?"

I replied, "About five minutes drive."

He said, "Right, answer my questions in the next five minutes and I will make up my mind - and could you please give me a lift to the station so I can get an earlier train back to Halifax?"

I was a bit surprised but agreed.

He said, "Okay, first question. What are the most important nuts on an engine?"

"The loose ones," I replied.

"You've got the job!" he said.

With that, he packed his briefcase to go downstairs.

I said, "Were you joking?"

"No," he responded, "I have already selected one man but the four previous applicants failed to answer that question - and it's an important one. You were the first one to walk in and answer it correctly straight away."

I said, "Well, it's common sense."

I drove him to the station so he could catch his train, he thanked me and then I drove home to Crawley, a bit bemused. I told Joyce what had happened and she said, "Oh well, you'd better start looking at the newspapers again."

A few days later, I received a letter confirming that I had the job, together with a railway warrant so that I could go to Halifax the following Sunday for a month's training.

When I look back with the knowledge that I now have, I can see that Spirit was working for me because it wanted me to have this job.

Six months after starting that job, we were called into the Manager's office. He told us that the company was being taken over and that the new management would interview the engineers over the next few days, to choose the engineers that they were going to keep on. The new company turned out to be Philips, and they selected five of us stay on. Philips paid twenty five per cent over the average salary, but they wanted a hundred per cent commitment back. Two of my colleagues were not prepared to give it, so they had to go. Three of the other five colleagues later left for a variety of reasons. I worked for Philips for two years; I dedicated myself to the task of being a service engineer and I thoroughly enjoyed the job. The job consisted of going out to people's homes and other establishments and mending Philips appliances.

*****

One day I was called to a job at Dorking in Surrey, at a place that was described as a Psychiatric and Psychologists' Office. While I was filling in the paperwork and working out the bill, the lady offered me a coffee and we chatted for a moment. She asked me how I liked the job and I told her that I enjoyed it, to which she said that was obvious from the way I had been working. I then told her that there was one thing that had been puzzling me since starting the job and that being a psychologist, she might be able to give me an answer. I told her that on many occasions, the lady of the house would get into conversation with me and tell me things that were obviously private matters. I told her that I rarely said anything about this as it went into one ear and out of the other, because none of this was any of my business, but I have wondered why they did this to a perfect stranger.

She said, "There's your answer - the perfect stranger. They need to get something off their chest, and you're not concerned with it - also you give off an aura of confidentiality. There is a feeling that you would never repeat what they tell you."

"Well, I'd never think about doing so because it's private to them."

She then made a comment that was strangely similar to that of the monk in Ceylon. This was, "You've got a nice gift. Look after it."

CHAPTER SIX

Illness, stress and problems

My work took me back to London, so we moved back there. A few months later, I began to experience pain in my spine, so I went to a doctor. This was a stressful time because only six weeks after moving to London, Joyce decided that she did not like it and wanted to move back to Crawley. We contacted the Council and requested a house exchange. Surprisingly within a matter of six weeks we got one and we moved back to Crawley. Apparently, it usually took months for these exchanges to go through, so we were lucky to be able to move so quickly.

My spine bothered me so much that I was referred to a hospital. The doctors there said that I had "blind boils" and that these would have to be lanced periodically to keep my blood clean. One morning, I was driving through Redhill in a line of eight cars - one of which was a police car. A driver shot out of a turning from the right and tried to cross to the other side of the road, ending up hitting every one of the eight cars on my side of the road, including mine. He not only dented the vehicles, he also ran into a brick wall at the end of the line of cars. By now, we had all stopped. The policeman got out of his car, went to the crashed car and pulled the driver out. The man was drunk - at eight forty-five in the morning!

The policeman radioed for ambulances to collect all the people who had been involved in the accident and arranged for us to be taken to Redhill Hospital to be examined. We were all shaken up but there did not seem to be any serious injuries. When the doctor came to me he looked around the area that was covered by the plaster on my back and started prodding it.

He asked, "What's this?"

"Well, according to Dalton Hospital, I have blind boils," I replied.

"Can I take a closer look?" he said.

"Be my guest," I replied.

He took the dressing off and did a bit more prodding.

"Sorry," he said, thoughtfully, "I don't agree. I would like you to stay here because there is someone else I want you to see this afternoon."

The policeman who had been present during this time asked the doctor if I was to be detained.

The doctor replied, "I'm asking him to stay. Why?"

"That's all I wanted to know," said the policeman.

He took my name and address and said, "Now, I can throw the book at that drunken driver - you've been detained in hospital and that's all I needed."

I said, "But I've..."

"I don't care about the circumstances. You've been detained and that means that I can throw the book at that drunk."

I turned to the doctor and asked, "What's the score?"

All he said was, "I've made an appointment for you to see a Mr. Stephens at one forty this afternoon."

I telephoned my boss. He was a very clever man and a very astute person and more intuitive than he cared to admit. I also know now that this was Spirit working for me once again.

*****

Mr Stevens said that my condition was definitely not blind boils. He arranged a number of tests for that afternoon, and told me to report back to his office when they had been completed. Later on, I returned to Mr Stephens.

"What's wrong?" I asked him.

He replied, "Well, you need to be admitted to hospital as quickly as possible."

"What for?"

"You need an operation for a growth on your spine."

"You're telling me I've got cancer?"

"Yes and you have a month to make your mind up whether to have this operation or not."

"Why a month?"

"Because, even with the operation, I feel that it will return within five years and then there will be nothing more that we can do."

He gave me the telephone number for Guy's Hospital in London and told me that I had to speak to his secretary to tell her whether I wanted to have the operation or not. He also said that he would not operate on the spine until the end of August or September when the weather was cooler and I would be more comfortable lying around covered with blankets while I got over the operation. I told the secretary before I left that I would have the operation and arrangements were made for me to have it done at Redhill.

*****

The combination of job changes, house moves, debts caused by having to furnish the first Crawley home, children and worry had got to me. Troubles either bring couples closer together or they don't - and in our case they were clearly causing problems within our marriage. Worse still, something told me that my wife was not quite the faithful girl I thought her to be, but she assured me that nothing was wrong and that things would work out for us. I returned home from the hospital visit and told Joyce everything that had happened there. She asked when the operation was due to take place and I told her that I wouldn't know until I received a letter giving me the date. I went back to work the next day and told my governor the score.

He said, "No problem. Your work has been good, so I will give you time off for your operation and I will also recommend that you receive basic pay to cover the time while you're off sick."

This was actually part of the Philips contract at that time and not a favour - but out of politeness, I thanked him.

I had the operation on the second of September. When I woke up after it, the first thing I remember was asking for was a cup of tea, and seeing my wife and children standing around the bed. I was puzzled because it was four o'clock in the afternoon. In those days, weekday-visiting times were between the hours of six and eight in the evening. I asked what was going on and she said it was Sunday! Apparently, I had been under sedation for five days to keep me still so that the spine could start to heal.

The doctor came in to examine me and said, "You're doing fine. I have removed a growth from your spine the size of my hand. The reason why you are uncomfortable is because we have placed support rods across your back in addition to forty-two stitches. You now must lie very still. You will remain in bed for three weeks on a non-residue diet and then I will see what progresses from there."

I was also advised by the hospital that I should wear a medic-bracelet, as my blood was rhesus negative. This meant that I could not have a transfusion should I ever require one, only the plasma solution. Around about teatime, my wife and children left, promising to return.

Two weeks later, Joyce sent a message telling me that she did not want me to return home. She had been told that I was liable to be sent home in a wheelchair, and she had said that she didn't think she could cope with this - not with three children to care for. It took me quite a while to come to terms with the shock of that. I stayed in hospital for another three months, and I had to learn to walk again because of the change in my spine. I also needed to get my bowels working again.

When I could walk again - albeit with the aid of sticks - I was ready to go home. The hospital tried to contact Joyce to ask her to bring my clothes and to take me home, but she had not responded to any messages. Messages were sent via our next-door neighbour, who had a telephone, and the hospital had also written to my wife, but she had not answered any of the letters. My bed was now needed for someone else, so they sent me home by ambulance. When I arrived at my house, there was nobody home and my keys were still inside, so I couldn't get in. I thought that perhaps my wife had popped out to do some shopping, and I waited outside for over an hour until one of my neighbours from across the road came over and asked if I would like a cup of tea.

I accepted but asked for a coffee instead, as one of the after-effects from the operation was that I became allergic to tea. Even now, if I drink tea I become sick. Another after effect is that I cannot stand and look up at a tall building. If I do so, I fall down, because the operation "moved" my centre of gravity. Never mind, these things can be overcome.

The neighbour told me that my wife had left the house a few days earlier and that nobody had seen her since. I said that needed to use a telephone and the neighbour took me across the road where there was a telephone that I could use. The amazing thing was that until then, I had only ever passed the time of day with these helpful neighbours.

I telephoned the local Housing Office and asked them to bring me a spare key so that I could get into the house, as all my keys and belongings were inside the house. They told me they would send somebody immediately but the person only deigned to turn up four hours later! The neighbour who had taken me in needed to go out, so I spent most of the time sitting on the wall outside my house. I was lucky that it was a nice day. Once inside, I made myself a meal and sat down to rest and relax. Nobody came. I was at a loss as to what to do. There was no note, no letter. Nothing.

CHAPTER SEVEN

I discover spiritual healing

Looking back on the whole incident, I now realise that if I hadn't been in that road accident in Redhill, my cancer would not have been picked up in time and I would not have survived. It is hard to understand why I had to suffer this sickness, operation and its after effects. In the event, it was probably meant to be, as this event, its aftermath and the subsequent ending of my marriage all transpired to turn me onto a completely different path than I would otherwise have taken.

*****

At about ten o'clock the following morning, the doorbell rang, and when I opened the door, I found a friend standing there.

"Come on mate," he said, "I'm taking you to see a pal of mine."

I was totally confused by this, and said, "But...where, what do you mean?"

"Come on," he replied.

"But I can't sit on a seat that has a back on it."

"Well, you can sit on this one because I fitted a handle to my dashboard last night."

My friend took me to a village just outside of Horsham and stopped outside a cottage. He got out of the car and I staggered after him on my sticks. I had made the supreme effort to teach myself to walk on sticks because I knew that my wife hadn't wanted to deal with a man in a wheelchair.

My friend walked straight through the open gate towards the cottage, walked right in through the front door and then called out, "George, it's me."

I followed him, not at all sure what was going on. We went into a little room at the back of the cottage and found an elderly gentleman seated in a wheelchair. He looked up as I came in the door and said, "Ah yes, I've been waiting for you!" and then, more mysteriously, "You can do it for yourself."

By now, I was beginning to wonder whether, on top of all my other troubles, I had gone through the looking glass into cloud-cuckoo land.

"Do what?" I asked.

"Heal yourself," he replied. Then he went on to explain. "I'm a healer and your friend has brought you to me because he thinks I can help you."

He began to talk about Spirit and healing, and it suddenly dawned on me that he was repeating all that my grandmother had told me when I was sixteen. The pattern that George used in that session is one that I have pretty much followed since, although some intervention from Spirit has caused me to adapt it a little over the years.

*****

I sat down on a stool in front of George with my back to him. He started by putting his hands on my shoulders and I heard him muttering. I assumed that he was saying a prayer of some kind. He then worked his hands slowly and gently down my back. Wherever his hands touched me, a terrific amount of heat emanated from his hands. I noticed that the heat intensified when he was in the area of my spine that was below my waist - and particularly in the area where the growth had been. When he did this, the pain in my back eased. I was trying to do a lot of walking to get my muscles working again after spending nine weeks in a hospital bed, so my muscles were quite painful at that time.

George reached the base of my spine and then moved across to work on my thighs. George himself was in a wheelchair because he could not move his own legs from the hips down, but he managed by moving his chair around and getting me to move around as well. He then asked me to sit down on the chair again, and he then went back to my shoulders and finally he put his hands on either side of my head.

I still remember to this day that George said that no healer should touch the top of a person's head, which is where the "crown chakra" is positioned. He said that it was possible to work around it but never across it because the healer could end up giving the patient the king of all headaches. George moved around my head with one hand on my forehead and the other hand on the back of my head, then he moved to the sides, across the temples and then back again - still mumbling all the time.

This routine was the same each time I visited George, and I always felt utterly relaxed when he had finished. George then told me that once I returned to work I would not need him again, but that if I felt any discomfort, all I needed to do was to sit quietly and think of him, and his "friends" would come along and help me.

The three of us talked and talked. My biggest surprise was the good friend who had taken me to see George. He was the Deputy Head of the local grammar school, and I had no idea that he had any knowledge of Spirit or healing... but life is full of surprises! George told me that he wanted to see me every week and my friend said that he would arrange to get the time off from his job so that he could bring me to him. George also told me to start driving again as soon as I could. Needless to say, this episode gave me a lot to think about.

I did lot of walking in order to strengthen my back and spine to get everything working properly again, and over the following weeks my friend took me for regular visits to George.

One day, not long after this, I was walking around the depressingly ugly centre of Crawley New Town when I suddenly noticed a sports shop. In the corner of the window I noticed a deflated swimming ring with the sun shining upon it. Quite out of the blue I had a vision of a swimming ring on my car seat. Puzzling over this I returned home. When I got back, I searched around for my son's old swimming ring, blew it up, put it on the seat of my small Bedford van and sat on it. Smashing! It took the pressure off the base of my spine.

I had occasionally started the engine to keep the battery charged but now I drove around one block. I realised that I was wobbling about too much so I drove back home and searched around in the garage to look for some webbing that I knew was lying around in there. I fashioned a belt similar to those on the seat of an aeroplane. I fixed it into the car seat, got back inside, put the belt on and I tried to drive again. It was great, I was no longer flopping around and it was ideal. Driving was the one thing that the Surgeon had said that I would never do again - but I was doing it!

My curiosity was getting the better of me by this time. Five months after the operation I took myself to the local library and began searching for a reason as to why George was helping me so much. I was clearly doing much better than the doctors had supposed I would.

At last I was fit enough to want to go back to work. I had made a point of taking a long walk every day and now I could drive. I visited my general practitioner and badgered him to allow me to return to work. He said the only way I could return to work was if the company doctor took responsibility for me. I made an appointment with the company doctor and then drove to Croydon on the appointed day. The company doctor examined me and said that I had obviously been doing as I was told, and agreed that I could return to work, but only on light duties. He immediately phoned through to Mr Ward at the service office. The doctor told him that he would allow me back to work but only on light duties. Bill Ward replied that he would have me back under any duties because he needed my expertise, and he said he was looking forward to seeing me again.

I started to leave the office, thanking the doctor very much when he said, "Hang on a minute, your job's in servicing. How are you driving?"

I said, "Well, I'm managing okay."

The doctor said he wanted to see for himself, so we both went down to the car park where I showed him the improvisations that I had made. He laughed his head off.

He said, "Right, we're going back upstairs."

"Oh dear," I thought, "he is going to stop me from going back to work'."

He said, "I'm going to make a phone call and you are going to have to wait awhile, so go to that window over in the corner and smoke your pipe."

I went to the open window in the corner, lit my pipe and sat there for about half an hour. Then there was a knock at the door and a courier came in and handed the doctor a parcel.

The doctor said, "Okay, you can come over now."

I went to his desk and he opened the parcel. Inside was a heavy-duty rubber ring, the kind used in hospitals for people getting over operations similar to mine.

"Right," he said, "Fit this to your car seat and when you can sit without it, I'll have it back."

I said, "Fine, but what's wrong with the one I've got?"

"It's a kiddie's swimming ring and one day it will burst, and I would hate to think what would happen then, as your spine is still healing."

So that was how I made it back to work.

*****

The day after I had been to see the doctor, my wife turned up with the children. It appeared that she had been living in Littlehampton with a boyfriend. Now she told me that her affair was finished and that she wanted to come home where we could pick up where we left off. I was prepared to give it a try, but as is usual in these cases, it did not last long. I still couldn't trust her and we argued about it. I believed that sooner or later she would go off again. I also told her that the boyfriend she had supposedly finished with was still hanging around. She denied this.

To be honest, I had been aware that there was someone else in the picture for some years, but I was still prepared to give our marriage another try. I guess that I was brought up to believe that, "when you made your bed then you must lie on it", and you either correct mistakes or live with them. Nevertheless, the marriage soon came to an end.

Some thoughts on the topic of healing and healers

Over the years I have seen healers do many strange things, such as waving their hands around to "clean" the air. Some tell their patient that they must sit in a certain position or move their hands and arms in certain ways, or that they must sit with their hands in their lap cupped upwards towards Spirit. None of this is necessary. Spirit actually does all the work, and what it wants is for you to contact the person's body at the right places - which are not always where the actual pain is. I have learned over the years to focus my work in the areas of the body where Spirit directs me. Sometimes the patient will comment that the area is not the one that is causing them pain, yet after the healing the pain disappears. I feel that Spirit seems to take me to the source of the problem rather than the area where the patient is actually feeling the pain.

CHAPTER EIGHT

A madman and an important visit to a Spiritualist Church

While I had been off sick, the supervisor had apparently been caught with his fingers in the till, so when I arrived back, Bill Ward made me the new supervisor. This was obviously the "light duties" that he had in mind when he had spoken to the doctor. My job consisted of checking complaints and monitoring the machinery and the work of the engineers.

One day, Bill and I went out to check on a large job. When we returned to the office, we saw Mary, the office secretary, pulling a face and holding the telephone at arm's length. We could hear a loud voice rattling out of it. Bill suggested that I deal with this one. I asked Mary what the problem was, and she replied, "Squadron Leader Kennedy."

"Oh dear!" I exclaimed.

Bill asked, "What's this?"

I explained to him that this was a difficult customer. If the Squadron Leader didn't have his complaint dealt with; he would be back on the phone again to Mary every hour until it was. Bill asked where he lived and I told him it was Wokingham, near Reading. He told Mary to put the call through to him.

The call came through and Bill said crisply, "Is that Squadron Leader Kennedy? Well this is Colonel Ward - good day!" With that, he put the phone down.

I gaped at Bill and asked, "What are you saying?"

He replied, "I'm a retired Lieutenant Colonel, but who the heck needs to know?" He shook his head sadly, saying, "You know, I can't stand people like that."

I agreed that Kennedy always gave the engineers a hard time. He complained about inefficiency and often said that he wished that we had been under him when we had been in the Services. Bill said that he had met a few people like him, but told me that I still needed to visit him the following day to discover what his complaint was. He told me to let Mary know that I was going to see the man, but that if he phoned again, Mary was just to acknowledge him and then hang up the phone.

When I commented to Bill about his rank, he said, "Why should I broadcast what I have been? I don't want to be known as Colonel or whatever; I just want to be known as Mr Ward, Service Manager."

*****

I went to see Squadron Leader Kennedy the next day to find out what his grouch was. It turned out that the engineer who had been sent to him had repaired his washing machine, and as per the regulations, had cleaned it before putting it back in place. This madman's complaint was - believe it or not - that a thumbprint had been missed on one corner when the engineer had cleaned the machine! Everything else was spotlessly clean except for this thumbprint.

I cleaned and tested the machine again and put it back into place. I made out the docket and gave the man a copy, but meanwhile he was going on and on as to how he was going to sue the company in general and Mr Ward in particular for misrepresentation. I told him that he would lose. He asked me what I meant by that. I said that my boss was a retired Lieutenant Colonel from the Army, which I believed was next in rank to a General. He said that he would "see about that". On my way back home I telephoned Bill to let him know I had cleared the problem and Bill said that he would see me in the morning.

Just outside Reading, I spotted a sign for a Spiritualist Church. I followed my nose, found the Church and discovered they were holding a meeting that very evening. I found a place to eat and then waited outside the Church until somebody came along. This wasn't actually my first visit to such an establishment as I had visited one in Halifax some years earlier, but this is where I really began to take notice of Spiritualism and to listen, talk and to watch what actually took place. If the crazy Squadron Leader hadn't called me out over a thumbprint, none of the rest of the story might have happened.

*****

My first visit to one was back in 1960 when I was on the month's training course at the factory in Halifax. The course was tough as it combined practical work during the day with written work in the evenings. Indeed, some of the engineers gave up because they found it too exhausting. On the last day of the course, the day before I was due to sit an exam, I realised that I was tired and headachy from all the cramming, so I decided to go for a walk.

I walked around for a while, and then when I was on my way back to my digs, I noticed a little Church in an area called Sowerby Bridge, which is a suburb of Halifax. The Church was even smaller than a normal house and it had an old fashioned appearance with a peaked front, windows on either side of the double doors and a cross over the door. If I remember correctly, it was just called St Peter's - and I had no idea that it was a Spiritualist Church.

I noticed people going in and thought, "why not?" and followed them in. I thought that it would be nice to go to a service and I considered that it might even make me feel a little calmer. The Church was so small that there were only fifteen or sixteen seats on either side of the aisle. There was an altar at the end with two lecterns - and I admit that I questioned in my mind why there should be two of these. There was also a small organ at the side.

I sat down at the back and a lady came round with hymnbooks, which she handed out to the congregation. I actually started to feel myself calming down and the busy buzzing in my head begin to ease. I looked around the walls at the pictures and messages that were placed there and I thought it all looked a little strange and different. I had no idea at this stage about the procedure in a Spiritualist church, or even to be honest that this was anything other than a normal kind of church.

The service was similar in some respects to a normal Church service, but different in others. For instance, there were no cassocks or gowns, and although there were prayers and a sermon, there was also two minutes silence for healing. A gentleman then came and took the place at the second lectern. To my surprise, the man who had been conducting the service (who I now know to have been the Chairman) turned and introduced him and said that he would take the remainder of the service for the evening. I definitely didn't recognise any of this as a part of a normal Church service, but in some unexplainable way, it felt right for me to be there.

The second man gave a talk on the philosophy of life, and while he was talking, I felt my head clearing and a feeling of relaxation coming over me. The talk was followed by a hymn, and then the second man stood up and began talking to various people in the congregation. I sat there both intrigued and puzzled by these events because I had no idea what was going on - but I still had the weird feeling that it felt right. I then felt the presence of my grandmother around me, which also puzzled me. I heard the gentleman tell people the names of other people who were not at the service, and he also described what these people wore, what they looked like or what they were like. Then he came to me saying, "It's for the man at the back with the beard."

He continued, "I know you are new to what we do, but someone wants to say to you, my friend, that you are a healer, so why don't you do something about it?" He then gave me a couple of other messages that I recognised, and I thanked him. We sang a final hymn, a collection was taken and there was a closing prayer and then the congregation dispersed. A few people went to the front and I noticed that a hatch had opened and that tea was being served. I didn't stay on, but walked back to my accommodation, feeling somewhat bemused by what had occurred. I felt totally relaxed and I didn't feel that I needed to revise any more for my exam, despite the fact that I had intended to do so. I passed my exam the following day and then drove home in a brand new company transit van!

Very little of what happened in that Church meant anything to me at the time, as I had not yet had my own experience of healing. I asked other members of my family what they thought the message might mean, but nobody could answer, so I put it at the back of my mind. The meaning of this first experience only became real to me later when I began to understand what George, my first healer, had said to me and what I discovered for myself later when sitting in "circle".

I was actually given a very similar message when I visited the Church in Reading, but I was still very much a novice at that time, with much to learn.

CHAPTER NINE

The end of my marriage

By now, my marriage was going from bad to worse. I was asked to go to the Midlands to clear up a few complaints and I had to stay there for four days. I told my wife that I would be back in the evening of the fourth day but I finished my work a day early. When I walked into the house, whom should I find but a strange man?

I said, "Who the hell are you?"

The man replied, "I might ask you the same question."

The expression on my face must have been a picture. "I happen to live here," I said.

"Oh, you aren't supposed to be back until tomorrow - why don't you go away again and come back when you should."

I threw him out!

When I walked back into the house, Joyce hit me over the head with a cast iron frying pan, and unfortunately, I retaliated by slapping her face. It was nothing more than an instinctive reaction to being attacked in such a way, but the following week, I found myself in Court being fined thirty shillings. Joyce didn't even get a slap on the wrist for what she had done to me.

She then announced that if I did not find a way to get out of the house she would kill me; also that she wanted a divorce. While the divorce was going through, she accused me of having had an affair, but I told my solicitor to get her to prove it because I most definitely had not. I would never have messed around with any of the customers or take time out while I was supposed to be working. Such behaviour would have jeopardised my job and I would have been fired - and I liked my job too much. My solicitor asked me if I minded if he investigated the accusation and I told him to go ahead. He put a firm of investigators onto it and they called various customers and went to my office to talk to my boss, all of who told them the same thing that I had told the solicitor. Divorce proceedings went ahead and I did not contest it - I just let it happen. The divorce finally came through and I left the family home. I asked my son to stay in touch, but he didn't do so. I suppose I just have to accept this as being part of life, but it is something that still affects me deeply today. I applied for an Access Order and this was granted. My wife didn't comply with it because she said that she and the children had now made a new life and that I was no longer part of it.

I had to make up my mind whether to fight for sole custody of the children. At the final hearing on my access rights, the judge told Joyce that she either comply with the Order, or she could go to prison for six months. Next time my time for access came round, I went to the neutral house, as agreed upon as part of the terms of the Order. I found the police waiting for me. Apparently, my wife had gone to the police to say that the reason she was refusing to comply with the Order was because I had "interfered" with my daughters. I was horrified, but I had no way of proving otherwise. The police asked me if I had ever touched the children. I told them that I had helped out when they were babies, as being twins they both needed attention at the same time.

The police advised me that, under the law at the time, this could be misconstrued as abuse, but they advised me to go home and forget about it. I was extremely upset, so I went to the Children's Welfare Offices and had a chat with them. Although they were sympathetic, they agreed it was how the law stood and that it would be difficult for me to disprove the allegation. They also agreed they knew there was no substance to the accusation as the girls had never complained, and when they were questioned, they had affirmed that I had done nothing.

They told me that I could choose to fight for custody of the children. However, they reminded me that the twins were nine years old and that I only had six years to go before the "turbulent" stage (as one of them put it) and being that they were girls, it could prove to be a difficult time. In addition, the children would hate me for sending their mother to prison and they might use this to behave badly towards me.

I said that I needed to have a talk with my son. When I did so, he suggested that it would probably be in their best interests to stay with their mother. He was nearly seventeen and a responsible young man, so I respected his opinion, despite my feelings. My son promised to keep in contact with me and keep me informed. So, very reluctantly, I walked away.

Needless to say, I tried to commit suicide after this, but Spirit stopped me - at least that is the only thing I can put it down to.

A few reflections

This was the worst period of my life and it is one that I shall never be able to forget. It came to a complete head one evening when my sister-in-law and her boyfriend came to visit her mother. We were short of some particular item in the cupboard, so they asked me to pop out to a shop that kept late hours. I took my bike and went to the shop. When I came out of the shop, I saw my wife emerging from the pub opposite on the arm of an engineer who worked at the same company as I did. I watched them walk up the road together. When I got home I asked her about what I had seen and she told me that I did not meet her "needs", and told me that she wanted to be with the man who I had thrown out of the house.

I had not wanted the divorce. After a year or so I sat down and had a long talk with myself. I saw that I had spent many years being aggressive and rude to females - any female. I had treated them badly and despite the fact that when free to do so, I had occasionally taken up offers, had always ended up hurting the women in question.

I decided that this behaviour was not doing me any good and I had to try to put what had happened behind me, and to hope that my children would contact me one day somehow. Unfortunately, this has not yet happened, but I still live with the hope that they will. I have long since forgiven my family for what they did, but it is not easy to forget.

This was brought home to me when I was in Holland for Christmas in 2001. The medium I was staying with suddenly asked me at breakfast who Joyce was. I asked her which Joyce this might be as I know of two and both were "in Spirit". She told me that this one had mentioned that she was the mother of three children. The message was that she was pleased that I had forgiven her as this had improved what might have been a pretty dreadful karma. She also said that she was proud of me and of what I was doing.

This was also confirmed as recently as the 27th March 2002, by a medium that I consulted at Gray's Theatre who told me that my mother is also proud of me. These messages make all the difference as they make me feel appreciated - at long last.

CHAPTER TEN

Back from the brink

My "access" days for seeing the children were supposed to be Saturdays, so on those days my boss would give me a relatively unimportant job to do. He figured that it would do no harm if I had to come away from such a job early, while on those occasions when Joyce refused to allow me to see the children, I would have something to do to keep my mind off things.

One such Saturday, my boss gave me a job to do in Winchester. Before the Winchester by-pass was opened, the A3 used to go through the city. When one came into the city, the road formed a steep hill with a sharp right-hand turn at the bottom, and there was a ten-foot brick wall around this corner. On this particular Saturday I decided that I would not turn the corner but that I would drive the van straight through the wall. I sat back, folded my arms and closed my eyes. The next thing that I remember was the sound of car horns. I opened my eyes to discover that I was in the middle of the road heading for the Market Square. I pulled the van over to the side of the road, stopped and got out. I then walked back to the corner to take a look. According to the camber of the road, I should have gone into the brick wall, but something had turned the wheels in a different direction!

I completed my work and then went back home, all the time wondering why I had not crashed into the wall. After this, I started to take my spiritual research more seriously. I was astonished by the way that something seemed to be coming together. A postoperative examination had amazed the specialist at the hospital, because he couldn't believe how fit I was.

I managed to find somewhere to live whilst the divorce was going through. When my now ex-wife discovered my spiritual interests, she used this as a means of discrediting me. However, my divorce had come through and I was free to pursue my interests in peace. I began to realise that Spirit was helping me - at least until a fresh problem came my way.

*****

One day, I went into the office at work and my boss told me that I had to give up domestic work and either transfer to the commercial side of the company or look for another job. When I asked why this was, he said that the company's rules were that only married men could be allowed into people's houses. This may seem crazy today but in those days companies had the power to insist on this kind of thing. Philips was a Dutch company whose head office was in Eindhoven in Holland, and the Dutch Reformed Church was extremely strict about such things; this attitude permeated through to their commercial organisations. Needless to say, this came as a shock to me, but the boss gave me several alternatives and I went home to think about them.

The next blow was that I was told that I had to move from the flat, which was over some shops, and which I occupied at the time. New property owners had taken over and they made a stipulation that nobody was allowed to live in the flats unless they worked in the shops below. They told me that I was going to be taken to Court to be evicted and that I would have to leave. Sutton Council spoke up on my behalf and represented me in Court, but I lost and I was given notice to vacate. The Council gave me a temporary bed-sit while they found me new accommodation. So, what with the divorce, the change in my work and now this - which was all happening over a short period of time - I became extremely depressed.

*****

One Saturday morning, I filled the gas meter with change and I started to write some goodbye letters. I was in the middle of writing the final one when the telephone rang. The phone was a communal one that was in the hallway, so someone knocked at my door to tell me that the call was for me. The man who had knocked asked me to be quick as he was waiting for a call. I picked up the phone and it turned out to be an old friend called Ollie who had given me a few lessons in clairvoyance and healing.

Ollie said, "I'm ill and need healing. Please come, now!" and with that she put the phone down. I went back into my room thinking that I could return later to complete what I had set out to do. I pulled on a pair of trousers, jammed a jumper on over the top of my pajamas, pulled my boots on and went out. Ollie suffered from some kind of ailment that came and went, so this was not the first time that she had called me. When she called, I would visit her and perform healing, make her a cup of tea and a sandwich, settle her down and make sure she would be all right before I left.

When I arrived, I found the door had not been left on the catch in the way that it usually was, so I rang the bell. Ollie came to the door and just stood there with her hands on her hips.

"What's the matter," I asked in some surprise, "you're supposed to be sick?"

She gave me a furious look and said, "I'm not sick, but you are! Get into my kitchen!"

I followed her into the kitchen and sat down, looking at her with some curiosity.

Ollie said, "Number one - I don't like my housework being interfered with and number two - you are not leaving this house until after we have been to the Church tomorrow night."

"But…"

"No buts. You can go home after the Church service tomorrow night. That's the instructions I've been given from "upstairs", so it's nothing to do with me. You are being stupid - you're trying to pre-call."

"If you mean that I was trying to kill myself, then yes. But how the heck did you know?"

"I received a visit. I was vacuuming when a tall, dark figure suddenly appeared in front of me. It was black from head to foot and it made me jump, so I switched the Hoover off and asked him who the hell he was. When he pulled the cowl from his head, I could see that he was a monk with a nice benign face. A white rope appeared around his waist, neatly tied. I asked him again who he was and why he was here and he told me that his name was Gregory and he was here to help me stop "our friend", then he showed me a picture of you showing me what you were doing. You were writing, weren't you?"

"Yes."

"And the gas meter was full of coins?"

"Yes, it was."

She told me that she had added two and two in the way that the Spirit had, and that was why she had called me.

Ollie then said that she didn't know what she would have done if I hadn't come, because five miles was a long distance for her to travel by public transport. She was thankful that I had answered her call.

"My instructions are to keep you here until tomorrow night," she added.

I had no choice but to agree. By then I had learned that if Spirit says something, it isn't wise to argue. Ollie dug up some men's clothes, which some ex-boyfriend had left with her, and sent me into her room to change. I took off my pajamas and made myself look reasonable. Later that night, I slept on the settee and the following evening Ollie and I went to Wimbledon Church.

As we walked through the door, I commented to Ollie that I couldn't expect to be given a message.

"Why not?" asked Ollie.

"Look who is on the platform," I said.

Ollie turned to me with a puzzled look and said. "Lee Lacey?"

"That's right," I said, "Lee and I trained together for a short period of time at Stansted Hall to do platform work, so he won't be coming to me."

The reason for my saying this is that it is an unwritten law that a platform medium doesn't go to the people that he or she knows."

"Hmm," said Ollie, "Let's wait and see."

When the preliminary prayers and introductions were done, Lee stood up and looked over to where I was sitting, "Many of you know I have a friend in the audience called Gordon, and he is sitting over there. Friend or not Gordon, I have been told that I must come to you."

He continued, "All I have got to say to you though, is that twice is enough. Pack it up because they will never let it happen. Do you understand what they mean?"

I meekly answered, "I do."

With that, Lee continued with his evening of clairvoyance and gave messages to other people in the Church.

Ollie looked at me and said, "Who wasn't going to get a message, then? I think that was forceful enough, don't you?" I had to agree with her.

*****

That experience cleared away any lingering doubts that I had about Spirit and the way that the spiritual world works. My grandmother's explanation and the strange apparition that I had seen as a youngster was one thing, but it takes experience of living and also that of working with Spirit, to develop faith - although all spiritual people still doubt from time to time.

Even today, I can experience slight doubt now and again, but when this happens, the words of the late, great Harry Edwards come through to me. He always said:

"Those of us who work with Spirit for the general public or for anyone who comes to us for help; whether it is for healing, counselling, readings or otherwise, cannot understand other people's suffering and we cannot help very much unless we have also suffered. We need the experience of life and of tough situations before we can understand those who come to us with troubles. Only then can we understand their problems, but it is also important to listen to what is told to us from the other side. That is the greatest faith - to listen to what Spirit says because, no matter what we see or hear or assimilate in our heads, we ask the question, 'Am I right' and then get the answer from Spirit."

The house in Hunstanton where Gordon was born.

Gordon's grandmother, Jessica.

Young Gordon is in the front seat.

Gordon with his mother.

Gordons father.

As an air cadet.

In the Royal Navy.

**Gordon at his
wedding to Joyce.**

Gordon and Russell Grant.

One of Gordon's spiritual guides.

Gordon in 2002.

Father Gregory, Gordon's main spiritual guide.

Heather, Gordon and his brother Jeffrey.

Another of Gordon's guides, who helped him with healing.

The BAPS committee in 1987.
Back row *(from left)*: George Dale, Janis Huntley, Betty
Nugent, Eve Bingham, Sasha Fenton.
Front row: Gordon, David Bingham, Renee Hindle.

At a BAPS gathering in 1988.
From the left: David Bingham, Sasha Fenton, Kathy Fay,
Gordon.

CHAPTER ELEVEN

A recap of my experiences of Spirit, and some advice - then on with the story

My first experience of the thin veil between this world and the next occurred on a night of heavy bombing during the early part of the war when my late aunt came to reassure me that I would be all right.

My first major experience, and the one that put me on the road to my later life as a healer and medium, occurred in 1963 when I was given healing for my cancer. This was not only a surprise to me at the time, but it sparked my curiosity as to what was happening to me and how it could happen. It was soon after this that I made my second visit to a Spiritualist Church on a journey of discovery and to see what went on in the Church itself. I then looked for books on the subject and started to study what others had experienced, along with explanations of the various writers' thoughts and their stories of the pathway to knowledge. At the time, I was living alone in a small furnished flat, which gave me the mental space that I needed in order to read, study and go wherever I wanted to go in order to gain the knowledge and experience that I was seeking.

I was living in a place called the Mansions, which were made up of a number of flats contained within what had once been a large mansion in the past. Two ladies who had retired from their jobs as company secretaries in the City of London had got together to purchase the Mansions. Curiously enough one of my landladies helped me at this time. Not unexpectedly at that particular time in my life, I was dreadfully worried and upset. I had not wanted the divorce and I missed my children and worried about them. I worked well enough but I couldn't sleep, so I would often get up during the night and wander around in the large garden. It turned out that one of my landladies was also an insomniac, so she used to see me wandering around. Sometimes she joined me in my nightly wanderings, and we would talk about my interest in Spirit. It turned out that she also had a similar interest. Sometimes, when I was mulling over a book I would give her a synopsis of the book or she would read the book herself while I was at work. She took the role of devil's advocate, putting various aspects to me that we would then debate - and this helped me to learn. Sometimes words would come into my head, which I now know were sent to me from another source. One such conversation from "elsewhere" said:

"Don't accept everything you are told. Only accept what you can accept and what feels right for you. It is not necessary that you believe everything you are told, but it is necessary for it to feel that it is right for you. If it is, then discard anything that has no meaning for you and take on board the things that feel right to you. No one speaks one hundred per cent gospel. Every book, every idea is someone's opinion, so what feels right for you is right".

Despite my problems I still acted as a listening ear when I went into houses and carried out repairs. To an extent, this went in one ear and out of the other because I had begun to realise it was only the person's way of letting off steam. I didn't analyse it that much, I just listened and then let it go, but on reflection I can see that I was being given an insight into the psychology of ordinary people.

After a year in the Mansions, I began to visit various Churches, starting with Guildford, then Wimbledon, Brixton, Balham, Clapham, Malden, Hackbridge and others. In some of these Churches the people were cliquey, while in others, the people were friendly, and they were happy to chat or to let me listen to their conversations. I went to the centre for the

Spiritualist Association of Great Britain at Berkeley Square and to Stansted Hall. I went everywhere to listen and to learn.

I began to realise that once you start working with Spirit (which I did by giving healing at Churches in Wimbledon and Surbiton); Spirit is always with you. Providing you work with truth and you do not set out to hurt others, your awareness grows.

My advice to anyone who is interested in spiritual matters is to start by listening to yourself and to others. Spirit is always there and the Spirits will become like friends to you. Spirits become your friends because you work with them, but you must always remember to work with the truth.

Some time in 1964 I visited a Church in Ewell Road, Surbiton and ended up going there several times because I liked the atmosphere. Eventually, a lady called Molly Williams asked me if I would like to join a Circle, and then she suggested that I join hers. She told me that this would take one hundred per cent commitment on my part and the only acceptable reason for being away was sickness or being out of town on holiday. I explained that my job took me travelling and that I didn't have set hours, but she replied quite firmly that if I were meant to be there, I would be there! I often went straight from my last job to the Circle at the Church, but I always managed to get there for eight in the evening. Somehow, the jobs always finished on time - although sometimes only just. This kind of thing has always worked for me, because if I am meant to be at a group meeting or a class, I always get there - regardless of whatever else may be happening.

Many of you who are reading this will think of Spirit guides and masters. I don't think this way. I have felt uncomfortable with the word "guide" from the moment I heard it and I could not understand why. Then I began to realise that even thinking about the word "guide" made me feel cold and uncomfortable, so I call these entities my friends in Spirit or just Spirit. Slowly, I began to realise how our friends operate with us, and how it will control certain circumstances for short periods of time in order to make sure that we arrive where we need to be.

Editor's note: I call my Spiritual helpers and advisors guides; others talk about guardians, guardian angels and so forth. Some people argue fiercely that a guide is not an angel and that there are different entities that should be called different things. Like Gordon, I believe that whatever makes you feel comfortable with is right for you.

I was with Molly for a number of months, and then one day I visited Wimbledon Church to see a particular medium that was appearing at the time. A gentleman who I had never met before came up to me in the waiting room. He asked my name and told me that he was called Bill Bromley. He then said that he wanted me to join his Circle, and he commented that this was because he had been told that it would help me.

I asked him, "What's so different about your Circle?"

He replied that his was a "Rescue Circle". He then went on to tell me about this kind of Circle, saying, "There are certain Spirits who, when they were here on earth had no knowledge of Spirit and who did not want to have any. They believed that they just go to sleep at the point of termination."

I now understand that there is no force imposed when one goes into the world of Spirit and there is no compulsion to do anything. There is freedom of choice, just as we experience on earth. God gives us the gift of freedom of choice and neither Spirit nor we can interfere with it. Spirit certainly avoids doing so. The Spirits may try and manipulate you at times if they feel you are on the wrong pathway, but you soon recognise this. There is no compulsion, so if someone insists that "when I'm dead, I'm dead. I just go to sleep and I wait for the trumpet call", then that is exactly what will happen to them. They will go to sleep when they die and they will stay asleep until the day comes, when for some reason they will wake up - much as we suddenly wake from a normal sleep.

When this happens to those in Spirit, they become so disorientated that they float around. Some try to get back to earth. It is my belief that this is where eighty per cent of ghosts come from. While they are floating around they suddenly see a light, just as we would if we saw a candle or a match lighting up in a dark room. Just like a moth, they will travel towards it and go on to the next world. Sometimes a person on this earth, who doesn't recognise that they have the gift of attracting these "ghosts" or entities to them will suddenly see one of these lost souls. The ghost will also come towards those sitting in the kind of Circle that I was about to go into.

*****

There were two mediums in the Circle who were "Clairseeing", and they sat at each end of the table. Around the table were five others who would supply the power as we linked up with our energies. One or other of the table-end Mediums would contact a floating Spirit and discover who they were, why they were there and what they were doing, and then we would all mentally speak to them. Sometimes, we would do it openly so that the others could hear what we were saying, but the communication was also carried by thought to the particular Spirits who had attached themselves to one or the other of the Mediums. We would then advise the lost souls what they were, where they were, and where they should go. We would tell them, "Look for a light, look for a door where there is a light behind it, or something like a searchlight beam shining in the distance, and go towards it." When the soul reached the light, they would find someone who they had known, and who was waiting to help them.

One strange thing that I learned in that Circle is that not all the souls that were floating and disorientated were actually dead! Occasionally someone who was troubled here on earth needed help. Their Spirit would travel at night when they were asleep and they would come and talk to one of us, and at this time we would help them and give them suggestions as to what to do. It was impossible to actually tell them what they should do, as Spirit will not allow us to instruct others, but only to offer suggestions. It is then up to the individuals to make their choices, which brings us back again to the freedom of choice. You may hear from the person that you have helped or you may not, you just hope that the advice you have given has done some good.

*****

After meeting with Bill Bromley, I went to Molly and told her what I had been invited to do. She was pleased and said that she felt it was time for me to move on. I did not understand what she meant, but she explained that I had been invited to join this other group because Spirit had arranged it and that I would no longer be able to continue with her. I was a little surprised at this and protested that I was learning so much from her. She told me that, nonetheless, I had to make a choice. I could either continue to sit with her or move on to the Rescue Circle. She asked me who was running it and said that she recognised the name. I asked her if she could advise me, but she said she could not. She told me that it had to be my choice, but that if I chose to go to the other Circle, I would do so with her blessing, because Spirit had directed me to it. I said I would have to think about it and asked her if she minded if I made one visit to the other Circle before I made my mind up. She agreed, provided it was only one visit.

The following Friday I went to Bromley - once again, my work was finished in time. I arrived at the address I had been given. Little actually happened; Spirit may have arranged this for my benefit, being that I was a newcomer. It appeared that I had replaced someone who had fallen ill and could not sit anymore. I sat and I learnt about the "transfer of energy" that occurs between each member when you are helping each other in a group. It is a weird feeling. You feel a little tug in your solar plexus, but once you know what this is, you learn to accept it. I enjoyed the evening and realised that this was what I would really like to do. The following Monday, I went back to Molly, described the evening's events and told her that I would like to join the Rescue Circle. She told me that I would go with her blessing and that I would not see her again, except in Church.

CHAPTER TWELVE

The man who wanted his breakfast

While in the Rescue Circle there was one particular experience that occurred which shook all of us - although it was not such a surprise to Billie (Mrs Bromley), the Medium who sat at one of the end of the table. Billie said she "had a voice" - meaning that she could hear a voice in her head. So we all concentrated and listened hard - and then Billie gasped.

She said, "I don't believe this, but it must be right because I have just checked with my 'friends'". (It was during this time in the Rescue Circle that I learned that the sitters called those in Spirit their friends.)

Billie continued, "My friends tell me that we have picked up on a man who wants his breakfast!"

We had tuned into a man's voice. It took us quite a while to understand what he was saying because to begin with he talked in a language that sounded quite foreign, but with a few words that we could recognise. We soon realised that he was talking in some ancient form of English. One of the sitters, a man called Ted, was something of a historian, so he explained to us what was being said.

It appeared that the man was in a dungeon, and according to him he was hanging in chains on the dungeon wall. He was waiting for the jailer to bring his breakfast, which consisted of bread and water. All he kept saying was that he wanted his breakfast. We managed to start a conversation with him, although it took a while, because at first all he wanted was his breakfast. It took a couple of hours to get a dialogue going with him. It transpired that he had been a thief, and the Squire of the castle had put him in chains in the dungeon as punishment. He did not know how long he was likely to be there, but he knew he had already been there a long time. Towards the end of the evening, he suddenly "shut down" telling us that he didn't want to talk anymore.

This does happen sometimes, and under those circumstances, you just cut adrift and make a note of the person in Spirit, so that you can call them back at another sitting. However, the man in the dungeon had told us that he had seen the light but that he had thought that it was coming from the jailer's torch. The following week we decided to "call" our friend in the dungeon. We had no idea of his name. Billie called him and told us that he was back, and that he was still asking if we had got his breakfast. Though this time he seemed prepared to talk, so we explained to him who and what we were. We wanted to verify what he had told us about being hung in chains on a wall, so we asked him what year it was. He said "It is the year of our Lord 1136".

Astounded by the early nature of this date, we all looked at each other. We told him that he was not going to get his breakfast until he went toward the light. He said he couldn't go anywhere because he was locked in the chains. We told him that he could step away from his chains and told him to look into the distance and asked him if he could see another light.

The prisoner said, "Yes, it's down the end of the corridor - and the corridor is a long one."

We told him to walk towards it. He still insisted that he could not do so, but we assured him that he could and this argument raged between him and us for a while.

Our Rescue Circle had two "helpers" in Spirit. These were two Victorian street urchins. One was a lad and the other was a girl who had lived on the streets in Victorian times begging for pennies. However, these two were happily over the "other side" but they enjoyed coming to our Circle to help us out from time to time. We spoke to the boy and asked if he could help us out where this gentleman was concerned.

He said, "All right, I'll go." And then we all clearly heard his Cockney accent as he said, "Come on, mister. I'll take you down to the end of the corridor to the light."

The prisoner told us that he would go with the child, because he trusted children, but that he had long since learned not to trust anyone else.

We felt that this was one of the biggest successes that we ever had. There had been no compulsion. The man had died in the cellar or dungeon but he had not moved on, and nobody had bothered to tell him that he needed to do so. He finally left us, although he did pop back briefly once more to thank us a couple of weeks later. He told us that he had now "gone over" and that he had found his parents, sister and friends waiting for him. This had been a wonderful experience of rescue and it was one that we all learned from.

I stayed in the Rescue Circle for nine months, that was until Billie developed health problems and needed to go into hospital for quite a serious problem, so sadly, the Circle discontinued.

*****

I joined the healing group at Balham Church where I was asked to work two evenings a week. I only did this for a few weeks, because one member considered that as I was not a regular member of the Church, I should not be there. To my mind, this shows a complete lack of tolerance, but this kind of thing sometimes happens; the only thing to do in the circumstance is leave and find a new group. All organisations need new blood from time to time, if for no other reason than the fact that over a period of time members leave - and if there are no replacements, the group dies.

I found another Circle, and once again this came about in a strange manner, which proves just how Spirit makes things happen when it wants to. I was attending Wimbledon Church because I liked the medium there. One day, I was in the anteroom after the service when a gentleman came up to me. He was a large man with a friendly face. He asked me if I was free to join his Circle, because Spirit had told him that they would like me to replace someone who had just left. So this was how I came to join Bob Bassett's circle. I then became a working healer at Wimbledon Church. I was beginning to learn quite a lot about Spirit during that time.

While I was working at Wimbledon Church, a young lady came in and asked if there was somebody who could visit her mother. Someone asked her why she could not bring her mother to the Church. She explained her father had died and that from that day on, her mother had confined herself to one room in her house and was refusing to move. The young lady had visited Spiritualist Churches before, so she was familiar with spiritual healing and she wondered if she could get some help for her mother.

Apparently, the doctors who had been to visit her mother had told the family that they would just have to wait for her snap out of it, but the young woman felt that her mother needed some real help. I lived a couple of miles away, which made me the nearest to the address, so Bob asked if I would go.

The mother, whose name was Fiona, knew nothing about spiritual healing, but she allowed me to visit her because her daughter wanted it. The daughter explained to Fiona why I was there and what I did in connection with the Church. She did not want me to touch her or give her actual healing, so I just listened - because that can often be a form of healing in itself. I discovered that her husband had been a man with a strong character and that very little was ever done in the house without his say so. His death had been sudden and Fiona was just totally lost without him. She was so used to him making all the decisions - even down to writing her shopping list - that she was completely unable to cope and that is why she had shut herself off in one room.

At the beginning, the son and the daughter thought this was due to grief, but as the days turned into weeks and the weeks turned into months, they realised it was something more than that. The poor woman was literally too frightened to come out of her room because her husband was no longer there. I left and went back the following week to see if I she would accept my presence again. Fortunately, Fiona wanted me to continue visiting her. One day she was not feeling too well and the daughter and I convinced her to sit on a stool in front of me while I did the "laying on of hands". She enjoyed this way of healing and agreed that I could do it again. The next time I visited her, before we had had much chance to have a cup of tea or a chat, she asked me if I would do the laying on of hands again. I did so, but she still wouldn't move from the "safety" of her room.

I called on my "friends" and asked if they would help me out on this one. I started to speak with her and I soon found words coming out of my mouth without my having thought of them. In this way I was also learning from the situation. Fiona accepted the words of Spirit and she began to get a little better. One day, I called on her but when her daughter let me in, she told me that her mother had a bit of a cold. I said it was not a problem. She then floored me by saying, "But - mum's in the kitchen!"

As I walked into the kitchen, Fiona ran back into her room. I followed her into the room. Her daughter came in with a tray of tea and coffee, and Fiona and I sat down and began talking. Fiona explained that she had started to take steps out of the room but she hadn't wanted to tell me about this. She then told me off for being too early, which made me laugh. I told her that I had been calling week after week after week, hoping that one day she would go for a walk down the road with me. With that, I received quite a mouthful! I gave her the healing and went to leave, when her daughter suddenly asked me if I was annoyed with her mother for her sharp tone with me. I assured her that I was not angry with Fiona and explained to her that it was all part of her mother's progress. Anyway, this was a healthy sign as it showed that Fiona was beginning to gain the courage to have opinions of her own and to state them.

*****

I was still doing my share of healing at the Church. We tended to work in pairs with one healer sitting in front of the patient holding their hands while the other would do the laying on of hands for the healing. It was a particular rule of that Church that we never worked individually without the Healing Leader's permission. The Healing Leader at that time was Bob Bassett, who also ran the Circle in which I was still sitting.

There are some people who find that when something good or wonderful is going on they feel the urge to destroy it, and one night one of these destructive people came my way. A young lady came and asked to sit for a healing session. She was designated a pair of healers from among the three pairs who were working. She returned again the following week and asked for a different pair of healers. On the third week, she came to Jimmy and me for healing. I had heard from others that she had also attended the Thursday evening healing session, but I had not been there on that occasion. When she returned the following week on the Tuesday, she asked to be allocated Jimmy and me again. She specifically requested that I perform the healing. I completed the healing for her and she got up and left. About half an hour later, our receptionist at the Church came in, and she asked me to go out to the anteroom. Jimmy also came out with me and we found the young lady standing there with a policeman.

As soon as I walked out to the anteroom, she said, "That's the one!" and pointed at me.

I walked over to them and asked what I was supposed to have done. The policeman told me that I was being accused of having molested the young lady by touching her in a private area.

I said, "I'm sorry. Absolutely no way."

He apologised but said that he had to take a statement. At this time, I asked Jimmy to come and sit with me at the table. The policeman said that he wanted me on my own. I told him that Jimmy and I worked as a pair and that I wanted him present. He reluctantly agreed and took a statement from me. In the meantime, the young lady had disappeared. I told the policeman how we worked and exactly what we did. He came into the Church and had a look. He watched the other two pairs working and then we all went out again.

He said, "Okay, that will be all for now. I will contact you, either at home or back here when I have more news."

I asked him, "What news?"

He said that he would tell me whether I was to be charged. I felt awkward about this, but at the same time I also felt surprisingly calm. I do not know why I should have felt that way, but obviously Spirit was doing it.

The policeman made enquiries, which revealed that the young lady had a habit of going to Spiritualist Churches around London, and that she had accused different healers of molesting her in order to obtain money. Normally, she took the healer aside and said that she would not press charges if the healer paid her. She hadn't done that because Jimmy had told the policeman that we always worked in pairs and watched our partner work, and that this had been relayed to the young lady concerned. It was proved I had been falsely accused of malpractice and the police took no further steps. The whole experience of this false accusation deeply affected me and it showed me how vulnerable healers and the like can be.

I did not let this episode put me off, as this work was too important to me. I continued healing and finally graduated via Bob's Circle, to become a fully qualified healer. In the meantime, I had also joined the Surrey Healing Association, passed my tests and gained my Certificate in order to become a qualified healer.

I discovered that Spirit would use your own experiences as a medium of connection or comprehension. Let me explain this. When I am performing healing on a person, they become like a machine to me. I see cogs, pumps and electrical circuits. This was what I was trained for in my daily working life, so in my head, a person becomes a machine and I can "see" where the faults were. I could then move directly to those areas that were affected. They were not always the areas where the patient was feeling the discomfort, but I knew instinctively whenever I located the source of the problem. It is a fact that one learns all the time - and I am still learning!

*****

Some Notes on My Researches

Here I would like to break off and tell you a little about my research and investigations during the early stages of my "career". At one Church, there was a man called George who had a habit of giving me quotations of a spiritual nature. He told me that, if I wanted to know more, I should meet him at the Ewell Road service station at six o'clock on any Sunday evening. Out of curiosity, I drove to the place he had mentioned on the following Sunday and I parked the car. I soon saw George walking up the road. He took me along to a small Church in the Ewell Road in Surbiton and we went in to the service.

At the end of the evening, George introduced me to Len Middlemass, who was the President and also to his wife, Peggy. George explained that I was new to Spiritualism and Peggy told me that I should read a book called "The Psychic Defence" which explains how to protect oneself. The following day I found the book. I then bought a book by Harry Edwards called "How to be a Medium", and also his book on healing and a couple of other books on the subject of working with Spirit. I bought one of Shirley Maclaine's books, in addition to "The History of Spiritualism" by Arthur Conan Doyle. I researched other religions so that I could understand them in case I was challenged in those areas.

I discovered that basically, most religions encompass the same principles. This is something that puzzles me today when I consider the clashes in the Middle East between Christianity and Islam, because both religions are so similar in outlook. I have come to the conclusion that it is human nature that causes the problems rather than the religions themselves.

I recently saw a medical drama on the television, where a woman was very intense about some religion or other and as a result she tried to prevent the doctors giving her seriously injured child a blood transfusion. The doctor told her that we must follow our basic principles, because God will forgive them. This "medical clergyman" commented that most people read the Bible while wearing dark glasses and they misinterpret some comment that was simply someone's opinion at the time of writing. This also makes sense to me, because the New Testament was all written long after the time of Christ and it must have included a lot of uninformed opinion.

Over the years, I have taken on board the ideas expressed in books that make sense to me, rather than swallowing the opinions of others one hundred per cent. I have worked to prove that the information that I have come across is true, and I still do this with any new information that comes my way.

CHAPTER THIRTEEN

Some memorable events

When I joined the complement of workers at Wimbledon Church, I became a Team Leader. It is a large Church and in those days had a large congregation attending the various events and demonstrations that took place throughout the week. Each Team Leader supervised a team of four people who prepared the Church for the particular demonstrations or events that were to take place during the course of a week. The Team Leader ensured that everything went to plan. There were four teams, so I was on duty one week in four. By doing this job, I felt that I was giving something back in exchange for the things that I was learning. During this period of my life, for once everything was going smoothly. I was still a service engineer and I was still travelling around, although I had changed my job from domestic to commercial work.

At this time, I had long conversations with various members of my family about my spiritual work. Some of them accepted it and some did not - but this happens in all families. My father and I had many discussions and he admitted that he could not accept the fact that the soul "went on" in the way I described, and that it did not seem right to him. He asked me if I could prove it and I told him I could not, although I said that I believed it, and so we left it at that.

After I had completed my healing training with the Churches and gained my Certificates of Competency, the Surrey Healers allowed me to run healing sessions at my flat one night a week. I became very busy, so I extended this to two nights a week. The surprising thing is that, however busy I was at work, I always managed to finish on time - sometimes only just. The sessions sometimes unnerved me. On more than one occasion, a client who I had been helping for a couple of weeks would walk in and say, "My doctor says I couldn't do this or couldn't do that, but I'm doing it now after coming to see you."

Something happened inadvertently that did worry me in 1965, when I made several visits to a client in connection with my day job. The house was the type that we called a "Philips" house. This meant that most of the electrical equipment in the house was manufactured by Philips. In such cases, people could take out what was called the "Philips Contract", which was a maintenance contract for all their equipment, so periodically we would be sent to these "Contract" addresses.

The occupants of one particular house were a man and his disabled wife. The wife asked if I minded if she sat and chatted to me while I carried out the repairs. When I had finished what I was doing, she gave me a cup of coffee while I completed the necessary paperwork. One particular appliance developed a recurring fault, so I went back several times. On one of these occasions, instead of the man of the house answering the door as usual, the lady answered the door. I went into the kitchen and the lady's husband followed me in. He looked at me from my feet upwards to my head. I just stood there and smiled at him because I wasn't sure what was going on, so I asked him what was wrong.

He said, "Nothing, but I wanted to see what you were like and what my wife sees in you because she always asks for you. Did you know that?"

I said that I had no idea, and that I just did the jobs that the office sent me out on. He then told me that she had been getting better ever since I had been calling.

He said, "She tells me that that all you have been doing is chatting with her."

I told him that that was all I had done, as she obviously liked to chat a bit and I didn't mind her being there while I was working.

He said, "No, but what else is there?"

I replied, "Nothing."

He continued, "There must be because she has been in that wheelchair for years, and every time she has attempted to get out she has fallen over, but ever since you have been visiting, she has been getting stronger. All right, she can't go down the road and go shopping like she used to, but... what is it with you?"

I told him what I did as a "hobby" (as I called it at the time). He said that he had heard about people like me and asked me again if all I had done had been to talk to her, and I assured him it was.

He then asked me if I would continue to call at times that were convenient to me and talk to his wife for ten minutes or so each time. He offered to pay me, but I told him that I did not want any payment as such, although he could contribute to my petrol occasionally if he wished.

I walked away from the house after completing my work and said a hearty thank you to my "friends", but I admit that I was puzzled. I realised that we are not always sure how Spirit is going to work with us and we are not always sure what the results will be. This experience made me wonder whether I was doing right or wrong, because I still wondered why I should be singled out for this kind of gift. I did not consider myself to be a particularly good person. Even now, I do not think I am particularly good or holy; I just try and do my best. If somebody asks me for help I will try and give it. We all have to live together and this is how life should be - with us all helping one another.

*****

I used to start my private healing sessions at seven o'clock and finish at nine o'clock. At the time, I lived in a three-bedroomed flat that had been converted into two bachelor flats. My neighbour, David, was the landlord's son. He was interested in what I did and he occasionally asked me about it, although being a teenager, he didn't want to do anything of the kind himself. He offered to let my patients in for me so that I wouldn't have to climb up and down the stairs. I had put some folding chairs on the landing for the patients to sit on until I was ready for them. One night, I had only just managed to get a cup of coffee and a meal before David started to show my patients up. The first was a woman who had been to see me before and the second was a man. I was halfway through the healing with him when my door opened again and the first patient came back in.

She began to complain to me about a dish, but I didn't understand what she was talking about.

She kept asking me, "Where's the dish?"

I let her go on for a few minutes, with the gentleman patient still sitting there, before I asked her what she was talking about. She said, "You call yourself a healer and you are a Spiritualist?"

I nodded to her.

"Then why haven't you given me the opportunity to leave you a donation?"

I told her I did not understand. She explained that she had looked both on her previous visit and this one for a dish, either in my room or out on the landing, but there wasn't one. She asked me why this was and if I thought I was too good to accept a donation.

The gentleman then stood up and said, "I agree with this lady. You should allow us to give you something."

I was unable to argue with them, so I went to my sideboard and took the fruit out of a small wooden bowl. I found a stool and put it out on the end of the landing at the top of the stairs and I placed the bowl upon the stool. I asked them if they were happy with that.

They both said, "Yes. Thank you very much."

I replied, "No, thank you. I did not realise I was depriving you of anything."

The lady said, "Well, you were. You were taking away our freedom of choice."

I ended up having to give both the lady and the gentleman healing once again in order to calm them down because they had both become rather agitated. I had learnt another valuable lesson, which is never to take away another person's freedom of choice!

*****

On another occasion, a woman asked me to go to Brompton Hospital to visit a gentleman. It turned out to be her husband, who needed an operation on his stomach. She asked if I would go to the hospital to give him healing. I said that I would, but only with the doctor's permission.

She said, "But I'm asking you."

I replied, "No love, that is something that I can't do without his doctor's permission. You ask the doctor if he minds me coming in to do what you have asked of me and if he agrees, I will do it with pleasure and I will also bring a colleague with me."

She subsequently obtained the doctor's permission, and I took a colleague along to the hospital with me. Her poor husband was very seriously ill, so I visited him regularly. After about three weeks, her husband was sitting up and clearly recovering from his operation. The doctor called me aside and asked me what I did. I told him that I just held the patient's hands, said a prayer and asked my "friends" to help.

He asked, "Nothing more?"

"No," I replied.

"It's just that he is recovering much more quickly than other patients with his problem normally do."

I asked him if that was a problem. He said that of course it wasn't, but that he was just curious about what I was doing.

He said, "I know what you are, but I have never experienced it before."

"Well," I said, "when you go to bed tonight, just say thank you, and my 'friends' will hear you."

"I will," he said, "And I will talk to you again."

The lady's husband recovered and left hospital. The doctor invited me to visit further patients of his and when I did so, he would come and watch me. My visits continued until that doctor was transferred. Sadly the doctor who replaced him wasn't interested in continuing the relationship.

I was still full of doubts. I did not consider myself a person of importance and I didn't understand why I should have this gift or task in life.

*****

My Brother, Jeff lived in North West London and worked as a highways and byways engineer. One day, he was with a gang of workmen on a particular road that had some subsidence. They were trying to find out what had caused the problem when one of the householders came out and asked them if they would like a cup of tea. My brother got into conversation with the lady, who mentioned that she had a son who was suffering from a tumour. Although he professed not to believe in what I did, he mentioned my name to her and explained that I was a healer.

The mother then contacted me and asked if I would call on her. The woman said that she could not pay very much, but I told her that I did not want anything because I always received payment in some kind of funny way for what I did. By this I mean that something always came my way, usually through donations. I told her that I could not promise anything but that I would speak to Andy, her son.

I visited Andy for a number of weeks - then he was admitted to the Atkinson Morley hospital in Wimbledon. His mother had obtained permission from the doctors to allow me to visit him in my capacity as a healer and Andy told others in the hospital what I was doing when I went to visit him. This upset the sister on the ward as she felt that Andy's mother was allowing a "crank" to come in and see her son - despite the doctor having given his approval.

A number of the other patients on the ward came to see me and asked if I would also give them healing. I said that I would, provided they had their doctor's permission. As they all appeared to have the same doctor in the hospital, I was allowed to conduct healing sessions for all of them whenever I visited the hospital.

This continued for a number of months. The doctor came to me one day and said that Andy's tumour was getting larger, but it appeared that I was helping because he didn't need painkillers, and he found this surprising. This also applied to some of the other patients, some of whom were actually improving. Sadly, it came to the point when Andy finally passed over. However, he passed quite peacefully, which gave comfort to his mother. My last visit to the hospital was at the doctor's request. Two of the ladies I had been healing had not been expected to leave the hospital when they were first admitted. Now it appeared that, not only had they got better, but also they had formed a close friendship in the hospital and they had gone off to live together.

All of this intrigued the doctor and he wanted to know what I did and how I did it. The most surprising thing though, was the Sister who had been so opposed to me. She came into the doctor's office and I expected to hear some sharp words from her. Instead of this, she came over, shook hands with me and apologised for her previous attitude.

She said, "I know now that whatever you were doing has helped the patients, so I won't look down on people like you again."

I left the hospital feeling quite pleased that Spirit had at least been able to prove something to that sister.

*****

I have a particular friend called Bill who lives in Cork in Ireland. This is a friendship that didn't arise through my spiritual world, so you can imagine how surprised I was when Bill turned around to me and "admitted" to me that he was a healer, and asked if I had any objections to this aspect of him. I told Bill I had no objections at all, because I was one too!

Bill was a self-employed small business adviser. Sometimes companies get into financial trouble and call in such advisers to work out where the problem is and then tell them how they can overcome it. Bill's work was diminishing because there was a boom in Ireland at that time, and small businesses were becoming more financially sound, while larger ones took such advisers on as part of their staff. One day, Bill phoned and told me that he was getting into debt because his work had virtually petered out. I asked him why he did not do healing privately. He said he could not do that because, like me, he refused to charge for it. I replied that Spirit was giving me the message that he could charge for his healing. He then said that he would think about this.

A week or so went by and he rang me up and asked me if I was still sure about what I had previously told him. I replied that I was being told, "Yes. It will give you an income and it will give you what you need." Bill told me that he had money saved that would enable him to cover his living expenses for three months and that he would give it a try. After a month, he rang me up. He told me that he had rented a room and done a little advertising, but that he had not had a very good response. He said that although a few people had visited and donations were reasonably good, they were not enough. I assured him that they would be. Another week or so went by and he telephoned me again. This time he said, "I don't believe it. I am being kept busy from the time I open in the morning until the time I go home in the evening. My donation box is giving me all I need. Thank you."

As far as I know, Bill is still working as a healer, despite the fact he has had some health problems recently. Spirit will always give a healer the work he needs, and this was exactly what Bill was receiving. He spent three days at a clinic in Cork City and two days travelling around to people in the country who could not get into the city. The donations always covered his costs and gave him the money he needed to live on.

*****

I remember another occasion when I was staying in Cork on holiday and Bill invited me to join him for a day's run. He told me that all he wanted me to do was to sit quietly and put out mental energy while he was working. We went to one particular house in Dunmanwey and when we walked in, we saw a lady sitting in a wheelchair. There were nine children in the house, varying from teenagers down to about five or six years of age. Apparently, the lady had fallen, injured the base of her spine and had been told that she would never walk again.

She was sitting in a very old-fashioned wheelchair that someone in the town had given to her. She told us that the health authorities were due to come and assess her and she was hoping that she could get a better one. Although she managed to do some housework, she badly needed some help.

Bill worked on her and she said she felt wonderful afterwards. She managed to stand up, albeit only for a few seconds, and she soon had to sit down in the chair again. The following week, Bill telephoned me and asked if I would like to meet him at Dunmanwey as he was going to the house again. He had visited without me once before, so this was now his third visit. While there, we discovered that the lady had previously enjoyed dancing.

On this occasion, Bill had only been working with her for about twenty minutes to half an hour (which is a bit longer than we normally spend on a patient) when he suddenly said to her, "My friends are telling me that you can stand up."

She said, "I know I can, but not for long."

"Not only can you stand up, but you can dance. Come on, put some music on."

The children put on some music and she shakily stood up. Five minutes went by and she was still standing and talking. Suddenly, she moved her feet and then she was in Bill's arms and she was dancing! Not quite a jig or a jitterbug but she was doing a waltz and she was dancing around the floor. She then sat down and she laughed and cried at the same time and so did we. That lady continued to improve because Bill kept up with his visits to her. Once again, this was the gift from Spirit.

So, you see, we always get what we need. Spirit is always there. I firmly believe that if a person deserves help, he or she gets what they ask for.

The Bible says, "Ask, and you will receive" but it is very important to remember that, to get any help from Spirit, it must be asked for.

Even those of us who work as healers don't get any help unless we ask Spirit for it.

Some thoughts on Spirit and healing

Always remember that, whenever we work with Spirit, we must ask for what we need.

When I have a patient for healing, all I actually do is to lay my hands on their shoulders and ask for help. I then allow my hands to move wherever Spirit wants them to go. I have a kind of routine, which means that I always finish in a certain way. Spirit will also use your basic knowledge of life or skills to teach you how to do it. As I am an engineer, whenever I put my hands on a person's shoulders and ask for Spirit to help me my hands start moving, but in my head I see a machine. I see the pumps, gears and crankshafts in the human body. This is what Spirit shows me. I might see a broken cog on a gear or that an oil pump is not working properly.

*****

The following example will show you something that never works. It sometimes happens at a church service that the medium on the platform is drawn to a person in the audience and the medium gives the person the message that he or she is a healer. The message might say, "You have the ability and you must do something about it." A week or so later, this person comes along to the church, and approaches someone saying, "You need healing. I'm a healer and I can give it to you." This doesn't work because the so-called healer has not asked his spiritual friends to work with him and he has not waited for the sick person to ask him for help. It is possible ask, "Are you alright? Is there something wrong with you?" but you should never approach someone and say, "You need healing, I'm a healer and I'm going to give you healing."

By taking such a bossy line, you usurp that person's freedom of choice. It is up to the sick person to ask for healing, a reading or anything else that you can give them. In any event, whether you think you can be a healer, a medium or anything else, you first need to investigate the subject and to train for it. If you are told that you have a talent for healing, you shouldn't simply take it as gospel that you can go out and do this, but you must follow it up with some proper training.

I firmly believe in what the great Harry Edwards once told me, which is: "We are all born with healing abilities, but it is up to us to choose to develop this, just as it is up to us to choose the way we live our lives."

Yes, everybody can be a healer, whether it is just by listening, talking, the laying on of hands or becoming a doctor, a nurse, a paramedic, an osteopath or anything else of the kind. These people are all healers.

CHAPTER FOURTEEN

I meet Ollie

An incident that comes to mind occurred when I was working as an Engineer and was asked to go to Plymouth hospital. At the time, I had a brand new company car. I was travelling on the A303 towards Somerset on my way to Plymouth. I was driving in the outside lane and doing about 65 miles per hour, when a car on the inside lane suddenly decided to turn right at the upcoming junction. The driver must have realised that she was about to whiz pass her exit junction, so she just went for it without checking to see if there were other vehicles around. She didn't notice that I was in her way. She hit the side of my car head-on and the impact pushed my vehicle into the central reservation. My car rolled and lost its back axle, amongst other things, before finally coming to a standstill on its base. By this time, there were no wheels left on my car.

Everything seemed to happen in slow motion and I guess that I must have been in a state of shock. Despite other cars still travelling by, apparently I got out of my car and started to pick up parts of it that had been strewn over the road. I don't remember any of this, because my next memory was of sitting in a garage, drinking hot, sweet coffee while a policeman asked the staff in the garage where the driver of my vehicle was. He asked whether the driver had been taken to the hospital or the morgue, as it seemed unlikely that anyone could have survived that crash. I overheard the garage staff telling the policeman, "Neither, there he is." and pointing at me. The policeman did not believe them at first, then he sent for an ambulance, but when I was examined later it was found that I did not have a mark on me. I was still shaking but I had no injuries whatsoever.

Looking at me, the only thing the policeman said was, "But this is the man who was brought off the road picking up the wreckage."

The garage staff said, "Yes, he was the driver."

I do not remember doing that. I telephoned my boss to tell him about the accident and I negotiated with the garage for a car to rent. I arranged for the retrieval of my tools and equipment from what was left of my car, because I intended to carry on to Plymouth to do the job I had been sent to do. The police kept me at the garage for three hours before they allowed me to leave, but as soon as I could do so, I carried on to Plymouth hospital and started work.

At nine o'clock that evening I had still not quite finished my work, when the hospital engineer suggested that I should go to my digs and return in the morning. Accommodation had been arranged for me a few roads away from the hospital. I drove to the digs and went to go straight to bed whereupon I suddenly developed an excruciating headache. I called to the two landladies and I struggled back downstairs to see them and asked if they had an aspirin but they said they didn't have any. They told me afterwards that I had turned very grey, so they telephoned for their doctor who only lived a few doors away. When the doctor arrived, he took one look at me and asked me what had happened. I told him about the accident and he sent me to my room immediately, following me upstairs. He told me to take my shoes off and he got me a glass of water. He took two brown tablets out of his case, told me to take them and to drink the water, and that if necessary he would see me in the morning. That was the last I remember until the morning. I was still dressed and stretched out on the bed but feeling much better. The doctor had obviously given me a sedative to ensure that I slept. The doctor returned in the morning to check on me, and he told me that he realised that when he saw me, I was in delayed shock from the accident and that sleep was the best thing. He was right.

The car I had been driving was in so many pieces that the insurance company wrote it off, despite the fact it was only six weeks old. The local garage had asked permission to for their apprentices to work on it, as this was a teaching garage for mechanics. They also asked the insurance company if they would accept it back once the work had been completed. The car was returned to me seven weeks later and it was the best car that I have ever driven. The apprentices did a wonderful and exacting job on it and it was superb. I could not get over the fact that I had escaped from such a serious accident without even a scratch on me.

One of the first things I had to do in my rebuilt car was to go back to Somerset to collect the remainder of my work tools. My boss wasn't happy about me taking an extra day for this purpose but he understood the need for this. During this journey, I kept asking the question as to how and why I had survived such a serious accident. It was obvious to me that I was being told by Spirit that I still had work to do. A lesson learned.

Ollie

During this time, I was in the Chair at the Wimbledon church, and at that time the church could seat three hundred people. One day, when it was my turn to be on duty, the President came to me and told me that there was a medium who was due to appear whom I had not seen before. He warned me that she was very good, but a little temperamental, and to be very careful not to upset her. Therefore, I trod very carefully when Olive Brooks arrived. I brought her a glass of water and we started the service. When we reached the clairvoyant period, I was sitting on the platform when Olive began her demonstration. Contrary to staying on the platform, Olive had a habit of walking among the congregation. I had been asked not to interfere with what she did, because that was her way of working. She started off on the platform and gave one message and then she went to three young ladies sitting at the front of the church. These women were obviously friends, and Olive took up a position in front of them. She went to one of the young ladies and told her that she had a child in Spirit by the name of Tracey.

The lady shook her head and said, "No." Olive carried on about the child and the woman said, "Could be, but I'm saying 'no'." Olive then said a few more things that the woman accepted as being right.

Suddenly I realised that someone was pulling at the knee of my trousers. I looked down to see who was pulling at me but there was nobody there. In my mind's eye, I suddenly saw a little girl standing in front of me. She was about seven or eight years old and she told me that her name was Gracie. She even spelt it out for me - G R A C I E. I thanked her and nodded and she disappeared.

Having been warned by the President to be careful, I didn't dare interfere with Olive's demonstration. She ended her clairvoyance session and returned to the platform, and we closed the service down in the usual way before going out into the anteroom. There was a tray with tea and biscuits for the medium and a coffee for me on a small table in the corner of the room. I went to sit at the table but my main job was to give Olive a chance to wind down in peace. She could decide whether or not she chose to mix with the others. While I was sitting there, I told Olive about the incident I had experienced earlier when on the platform. Temperamental was the right description! She blew her top and asked me why I had not told her before. I told her that the President had warned me not to interfere in any way with her demonstration. Olive said she would deal with him later! With that, she walked over to the three ladies who had come in for some tea, and spoke to the one to whom she had given the message. Olive told her that she felt the child's name was Gracie. The mother accepted the name and they had a chat during which Olive offered more information to the lady. Olive came back to my table and told me that I had been stupid not to say anything at the time. Then I left her, as I had to close up the church and leave it tidy. When I returned to the anteroom, much to my surprise, Olive was still there and she said, "Do you drive?" When I replied in the affirmative, she asked where I lived. "Good," she said, "you have to go past the flats where I live, so you can give me a lift home."

On the way home she said to me "I've been told off!"

I asked her why and she retorted, "For having a go at you. Spirit told me you needed to learn more. I run a Circle and right now I have a vacancy, would you like to join it?"

"I'd love to," I answered.

She surprised me by adding, "But I don't feel it'll be for long. You just have some rough edges that need to be polished."

I dropped her off at her home and drove on, thinking over the events of the evening.

I went to the evening Olive had designated for her Circle and she told me that she had been talking with "the people upstairs" (Spirit), and they had said to her that I was good at talking. She told me that the one thing she did not like doing was addressing the congregation, and she asked me if I would do the addresses if she did the clairvoyance. That was how we ended up working together for a number of years, during which time we got on quite well. I would transport Olive to wherever she needed to go to work and I gradually began to do some platform work myself.

Olive and I became friends. One evening I said, "Olive, my bookings are fading away, what am I doing wrong?"

She laughed and said, "Nothing, it's because they want you to teach."

I had never been invited by anybody to teach before, but it culminated with my going to a church in Croydon and on my first evening there I walked along the corridor to the medium's room to sit quietly before starting. I happened to be wearing a cross at the time. I used to wear a cross about two inches in size when I worked.

A man, who I had never met before in my life, walked out of the medium's room, came up to me and contemptuously flipped my cross saying, "You can take that off, we don't have these in this Church."

I looked at him and said angrily, "In that case, I don't want to be here." I promptly turned around and walked out.

As I walked past the secretary, Betty, at the door I said, "Goodnight!" There was a fifteen to twenty yard walk from the church door to the pavement, and as I was walking away, I heard this same man at the door saying to Betty, "Has the Medium turned up yet?"

She said, "Yes, he has, but you've just sent him home!"

He then realised what he had done and came running up the path and along the pavement behind me.

He was shouting apologies after me but I turned to him and said, "No, you've done it. Go back and do it yourself. I am not in any mood to work now."

I was absolutely furious at the man's behaviour, but then I started to feel a bit guilty, so I rang Olive. She asked me what the matter was and I started to explain. She asked me not to discuss it over the phone but to go around and see her and discuss it over a coffee instead. When I told Olive what had transpired, she just laughed and said, "It's the answer to your question the other night. Spirit want you to teach and tonight you started, because you taught that man to think before he acts." Olive then asked me to describe the man. "Oh, he deserved it", she said.

"Do you know him?"

"Yes, I know him. That was a lesson he needed to learn."

I told her that I felt a bit guilty and she said, "Don't be. No-one upstairs is blaming you - but this is the end of this type of work for you."

"It can't be, I've got two bookings left."

"I don't think so. Now, it is time for you to teach."

What Olive said turned out to be right because within the week, one of my bookings was cancelled because the Church I was supposed to be demonstrating at was temporarily closed due to a fire. It turned out that the second booking was also cancelled as they had double-booked and I told them to take the one they had double-booked with. Apart from my healing sessions during the week, it appeared I was now left with nothing more to do.

During the next three weeks I got seven telephone calls from different people who asked me to teach them. I had often been questioned after Church services but nobody had actually asked me to teach before. I then understood what Spirit meant when they said they wanted me to teach. I formed my first Circle and Olive and I remained great friends.

*****

There were times when in my engineering work, I would come across a problem that was a bit tricky and I would ask Spirit to help and direct me. I cannot ask Spirit to do my job for me, but I can ask for help as to where to look. For example, I may have been working on a control cabinet with a mass of wires, switches and transformers, but I would be given guidance as to exactly where to look for the fault. Nobody came into my head and told me where to look or to confirm whether I was right or wrong without my first asking for help.

One day when I was at work, I was making my way to the stores to collect some spare parts. There was a lady coming toward me who was normally full of the joys of spring. On this particular afternoon though, she had a very long and a troubled face.

As I approached her I said, "Hi, Diane, what's the matter?"

She said, "Oh, I've got the king of headaches. I can't shift it."

Without thinking, I put my hand up and touched the side of her head for a few seconds and said, "Never mind love, it'll be gone shortly" and carried on to the storeroom.

I did that without thinking. I did not ask for help from Spirit. I just did it. I then collected my spares, went out to my car and put them in the boot. When I walked back into the office, I heard someone scream, "Look out, here comes the Witch!"

"What does that mean?" I asked, along with everybody else who asked the same thing when they heard her squeal.

She said, "I've had a headache all day and I've taken tablets but I still couldn't get rid of it, then he touched the side of my head and now it's gone."

I said, "Oh, that was coincidence," and I carried on walking toward the Chief Buyer to hand in my order.

He then asked me in a whisper if I would come round to the other side of the desk.

"Are you a healer?" he asked, and I told him that I was.

His next comment took me aback. He said, "So am I. Come back and see me at five o'clock."

I went back later and we began to talk. It turned out that he worked at Balham Church while I worked at Wimbledon. People at work then began to find out what I did and from then on, I became known as "Holy Joe", and a number of other names. I was not upset by it, as it was only said in banter, and I was not in the factory very often, so it did not matter anyway.

Months went by and I was still working and performing my healing at home as well at the Church. I was gaining confidence but my abilities developed slowly. I also noticed other things beginning to happen to me and around me in the spiritual sense.

It was always our company's policy to lay on a Christmas dinner and dance for the staff. We paid a percentage of the ticket price. I didn't have a partner but I knew most of the people at the firm so I knew I would have the odd dance with one or two. Towards the end of the evening, everybody was putting on their coats and wishing each other happy Christmas because the firm was closing down over the Christmas holiday. This year, though, it fell to me to be on standby for any emergency calls, so I had to stay at home during the holiday period just in case.

While I was putting my coat on, Diane came over to me, threw her arms around my neck and gave me a big kiss - a big juicy kiss!

Astonished, I looked at her and said, "What on earth are you doing?"

She laughed and said, "My husband, Dennis, wants to speak to you."

I walked with her to where her husband was standing and he put his hand out to shake mine saying, "So, you're Gordon. I just want to thank you."

"What for?"

"We have been married for eleven years and throughout this time Diane has suffered from severe headaches. The doctors said it bordered on being a migraine, although I'm not quite sure what they meant but from the day you touched the side of her head, she hasn't had one. Why is that?"

"I don't know."

"What did you do?"

I told him that I had just put my hand up to Diane's head.

"Just that? What are your abilities?"

"I'm a Spiritual Healer."

Dennis then asked me if I would go home with him and Diane for a coffee because he said he would like to talk with me further. I accepted and we all drove back to their house and we spoke for half an hour or more. Dennis was very interested in discovering what being a Spiritual healer was all about. Dennis then kindly drove me home.

The following evening, I arrived home and sat down in my flat and thought, "Spirit, you are beginning to frighten me a bit."

I then had a beautiful feeling wash over me. I did not receive any kind of message in my head, but a wonderful feeling just drifted over me.

Then I heard a voice say, "Forget it - calm down."

CHAPTER FIFTEEN

Other doors begin to open

I was beginning to realise that other things were happening around me and I started to take a lot more notice of them. I had a friend called Christina Artemis who was an actress. She and I had sat in a Circle many years before, and she was also a good Medium. She decided to hold a Christmas dinner for her friends and she sent me an invitation.

I was a bit early and Christina was still involved with the preparations but while I relaxed in the lounge, Christina came in and handed me a package.

"Here you are", she said. "I've brought something special back for you." She had been out around Hong Kong, Singapore and the Far East with a travelling troupe who had been performing plays.

"I bought these for you as your Christmas present because I know you can do them!"

Perplexed by her comment, I opened the gift and it turned out to be a pack of Dakini cards. They felt lovely in my hands. Dakini are an eastern form of Tarot cards. Oddly enough, although a deck of cards is such a personal thing, it is amazing how frequently being given his or her first deck starts off a future card reader.

*****

I fiddled about with the cards, read the booklet and I sat with them until it was time for the meal, and then we all exchanged Christmas presents. We were relaxing over coffee at the end of the meal when Christina suddenly looked across the table and asked me what I thought of the cards.

I replied, "I think they're lovely. Why did you ask?"

"How confident do you feel with them?"

"I don't know yet."

Christina and her friends cleared the table, leaving just the coffee remaining there.

She then said, "Give us a reading, Gordon!"

Tentatively, I worked my way around the table, reading two or three cards for each person for a couple of minutes or so. I was surprised to find that people were accepting the things that I said, and it was then that I realised I was in the process of learning yet another skill.

I took the cards home and I studied them some more; then I asked my "friends" if this was what I should be doing, and they replied that it was.

This was the start of the development of yet another gift. I did not receive information in the form of a voice or an image. It was just that whenever I laid a card, there was information in my head that I felt that I had to impart to the person with me. I became reasonably proficient with them. As my interest in the cards increased, I bought myself a set of western and other types of Tarot cards and became proficient with those as well. I discovered that although I began to learn the accepted meaning of the cards, whenever a card was laid, other information came into my head along with it. I now find that the cards act like a trigger, and I have a "friend" who steps in and tells me how the cards apply to the client who is in front of me. Occasionally, I receive information that is not on the cards, but I trust it and the clients always accept this from me.

Trust is important when working with Spirit.

It is a fact that you have to do what Spirit wants you to do, whether it is healing or readings.

*****

In 1972 I received a phone call in the early part of the year from Christina Artemis asking if I knew where Acton was and asking me if I could accompany her there. This was the occasion when I met the actor, Russell Grant, for the first time. There were five of us who attended the Acton meeting at Russell's home that night and these were Russell, Chris Green, Reneé Hindle, Christina and I. We all had different classifications in the ways that we worked. Chris Green was a Ufologist, Reneé a Clairvoyant and so on. Russell announced that he wanted to bring a group of like-minded people together, so we arranged to meet each week on the same night.

For me, this was the beginning of a lovely friendship with Reneé Hindle. She was a gifted pure clairvoyant. Unfortunately, Reneé had a problem, which I know she would not mind me telling you about. If Reneé travelled only a mile away from her home she got lost! Even that night, she had problems finding her way to Russell's, so I offered to take her home along with Christina and this became a permanent arrangement thereafter.

As the weeks went on, the group built up until we numbered eight. We were all different and I was the healer in the group. Russell, with his connections in the theatre-world, had decided that he wanted to put on a demonstration. He wanted to prove that eight different classifications of work with Spirit could work together. There were many myths around (and there still are) that if you use one type of energy, another energy cannot work alongside you. What people fail to realise is that the energies that we use all come from the same source! It is only our adaptation of that energy that makes us different - but all the power still comes from one source, which is that of Spirit.

We put on our first demonstration at Putney Bridge. It proved to be very successful, we had a good audience and people liked it. One man there heckled us, but you get that wherever you go. He was not doing it rudely, but he heckled continually, regardless of what was going on. We held a healing session and invited anyone from the audience to come up onto the stage in order to experience it. The heckler came and sat down on the stool in front of me. I asked him if there was anything he wanted to tell me.

He replied, "Mind your own *** business!"

Ignoring him, I placed my hands on his shoulders as I normally do, asked my friends to help and went through my routine, thanking Spirit when I was finished. The man got up, thanked me and went back to his seat in the audience. After giving several more people healing, I became the master of ceremonies for a sketch that Russell had written. Russell performed the sketch, along with Christina, Chris Green and another lady called Anne Halfehide. The sketch consisted of the twelve signs of the zodiac with the performers displaying the attributes of each one of the signs in a comedy sketch scene, and this went down very well. Before the finale, Russell walked to the front of the stage and asked if there were any comments before the curtain was finally closed.

The man who had previously been heckling us stood up and said, "Yes, I want to know what that man did to me." Russell said, "I don't understand. What do you mean?"

He replied, "I came up to experience the healing."

Russell said, "Yes I know, do you have a complaint?"

"No, far from it. In fact, I've had a frozen shoulder for three years and now it has gone and I can move my shoulder about without any pain, so what did he do?"

Russell gave him a brief explanation as to how we ask Spirit to help us and that our friends in Spirit come in and do the work.

He said, "Well, I'm here as a journalist to report on tonight because it is something different for this area."

We all wished him well and he went on his way. Instead of receiving the bad publicity we had expected, we actually received a reasonable write-up. The reporter did not mention his shoulder, but he did give us quite a complimentary press describing us as

"A group of people who used their energies and skills for the good of others".

This publicity was significant to us because soon after, we all received a phone call from Russell saying that we had been asked to do a demonstration at a Gingerbread Club, followed by one for the Women's Institute, the Red Cross and so on. The more we did, the more we were asked to do. We also began to realise that despite the different venues, we often saw the same faces in the audience. Apparently a group of "fans" was following us around. Russell used to announce, "It looks like we have a few groupies!" but he said this in fun and this was always greeted with laughter.

The group was now firmly established, but we found that there were others who wanted to know about us, so we formed the British Astrological and Psychic Society (BAPS). BAPS is still very active today and is hugely successful. Among other things, BAPS provides certificate courses for anyone who wishes to learn one of a number of skills, as well as vetting for those members who wish to become qualified BAPS Consultants.

CHAPTER SIXTEEN

A death in the family, and proof of survival of the spirit

In 1974, I had a very profound experience. Before describing this, I have to go back to 1948 when my mother was sick. She was sat up in bed order to take a drink from my sister and fell back - stone dead. My father was asleep and we had to wake him to tell him what had happened. My mother's death broke him up, and it was nearly two years before he returned to a reasonable way of looking at life. I am the oldest of seven children. My brothers and sisters went their own way, but I made a point of periodically calling in to see my father. Over the years, we discussed my beliefs in depth. Pop had difficulty in understanding how - as he called it - I had changed my religion. I explained to him that I had not changed my religion but that I had just extended it. We had been a family of Anglo-Catholics, but as time went on, my father and I had many discussions over the years - which included the bible and so on. My father accepted my belief but now and again he would still want to talk it over with me. He frequently said that he found it hard to accept the idea of the survival of the soul.

On the 6th of June 1974, my father arrived at Jeffrey's flat in North West London at nine o'clock in the morning. This was utterly contrary to his usual behaviour, as he usually stayed in bed until about eleven o'clock. My sister-in-law, Heather, was not too pleased by his early arrival, but she got on very well with my father. While they would often argue they were always pleased to see each other and if one of them was ill or in difficulties, the other one always went to help. On this particular morning, my father was feeling peckish, so Heather went into the kitchen to make him something to eat. My brother had popped out to get some shopping. When he came back and saw our father, he stood just inside the doorway before taking the shopping into the kitchen, waved and said, "Hi!" My father said, "Hi" back and then he suddenly jerked and fell back into the corner of the settee.

My brother quickly realised that my father had had a heart attack and that it was fatal. He telephoned my place of work and I immediately went to my brother's house. As always, Spirit had made sure it wasn't too hard to contact me. I was not too far away because I was working at a hospital in London. My boss telephoned me and told me to pack my tools and leave. He said he had another engineer coming to take over and told me that I should go to my brother's house as I was wanted urgently, so I got on my way. My boss told me afterwards that he had told me that my father had died, but I thought that he meant my younger brother, Derek, who was very ill and in hospital at the time. Derek had been an invalid from the time he was born and at that particular time, he was back in hospital for a while.

I was so upset that I unknowingly drove across a zebra crossing while a pedestrian had his foot on the crossing and a policeman on a motorcycle stopped me. I had a few tears on my face and the policeman asked me what was wrong, so I told him. He asked me where I was going and I told him Harlesden. He told me to sit where I was for a moment and he went back to his motorcycle and put on his blue light - he then told me to follow him. The next minute, a police car pulled in behind me, also with its sirens blaring. They speeded up and escorted me. The motorcycle policeman then pulled up alongside of me and said that I would know my own way from here, I was to take it easy and that it would not be long before I arrived at my brother's house. The police left, I said, "Thank you Lord" and continued on to my brother's.

I was the first family member to arrive, and as I walked in I saw my father hanging over the side of the settee with his glasses hanging askew and his teeth hanging out. It was then I realised why I had been called. I was shocked, not only at my father's death but also with his appearance.

I said to Jeff, "You can't leave him like that."

He said, "I have to leave him because the Coroner wants to see him."

I said, "No way."

I went in and tidied him up, all the time asking Spirit to help him on his way. My father just looked as if he was sleeping peacefully. The Coroner arrived and asked me who I was and I confirmed to him that I was the eldest son.

He said to me, "Leave him with me and I will come and see you in the kitchen afterwards."

I told him that the house belonged to my brother. He said that he already knew that because my brother had phoned him, but once again he asked me to go into the kitchen to join the family as my other brothers had now arrived.

Heather made me a cup of coffee, but she seemed somewhat agitated so I asked her what was the matter. Jeff then explained that she was very upset because when she had walked in to the living room, carrying a tray with some food on for my father, she had thought that he had fallen asleep and she had had sworn at him. It took a few seconds before my brother was able to explain to her that my father was asleep - but on a permanent basis. She was now feeling upset and guilty.

It is peculiar how people react at such times. Jeff shook hands with me, because he had not done so when I arrived, but when I went to shake hands with my younger brothers, Michael shook my hand but Colin refused to because I had "touched a dead body". This, of course, being irrespective of the fact that it was our father. He was very adamant about it, but he did ask me what I had been "muttering" about. I told him I had been asking

Spirit to help Pop on his way, but Colin's reaction to this was "Oh, that load of rubbish!"

I telephoned my boss and gratefully accepted his offer of a week off and I started to make the necessary arrangements. I did as much as I could on the Friday, but some matters had to be left until the Monday so my brother said to me that I had better stay with him and Heather for a few days.

On the Sunday afternoon, Heather suddenly said to me, "Will you take me to Church? I want to go to your Church." I said that I would but I was somewhat perplexed because she actually attended a Church that was near where they lived. I pointed out that mine was on the other side of London, but she then said, "I don't know why I want to do this, but I do want to go to your Church."

On the way there, Heather asked me what she could expect and I explained to her that, basically there was very little difference to a normal service except for the fact that we held clairvoyant sessions. She asked me what that involved and I told her that she would find out when she got there. She asked me if I would receive a message and I answered, "Not necessarily."

When we arrived at the Church, I told her that I would definitely not receive a message but that she might. She asked me why I was so sure that I wouldn't be given a message. I explained that the man who was conducting the clairvoyance that evening was Lee Lacey and that I had trained with him, so due to that circumstance he would not come to me. After the service, the session began.

Lee worked around the Church for quite some time when suddenly the Chairlady said to him, "You can do one more, Lee."

He said, "I want to go to the man at the back with the beard."

I answered him but I was surprised that he had not called me by my name. Then he really surprised me because he began to talk to me in a Norfolk idiom - the dialect of my childhood. It came to mind that it could have been my father, but I dismissed it, thinking that it couldn't be possible. Heather thought right away that it was Pop.

After a few moments, Lee continued, "Oh, he's changed his attitude now, and he's talking to me in English. I couldn't understand that language before." Lee continued, and I found myself thinking that the message could be from Pop, although it didn't seem possible - until the end of the session, that is. Lee said, "This communicator wishes to tell me quite forcibly - and he wants you to fully understand, that he's proved that which he was always uncertain about. Do you understand what he means?"

"Yes," I replied.

"Well now, I want you to take another message from him. He says when he is buried on Thursday, put the fish at the front."

I thought then that it couldn't have been Pop because he was being buried on the Friday. Heather and I left the service, and because I was a member of the Church Council, I went into the medium's room.

Lee looked up and said, "Hello Gordon, where have you come from?"

Rather puzzled at his attitude, I said, "Lee, I was your last message."

He gave me an odd look and said, "No you weren't."

I asked him to describe the person who he thought the message was for - and he described my grandfather!

When I told him that he laughed and said, "In all honesty, I hadn't noticed you at any time during the evening."

He asked me what the "fish at the front" meant and I replied that I hadn't a clue. I went on to say that if it had been my father - and that was a big if - it had only been three days since his death. I asked him about the point that he had made about "proving a lack of understanding" and he said that he couldn't make any sense out of that either. I told Lee what my father had always said to me about "survival", and he said to let him know if anything more came of the evening's events.

On the Monday morning, we received a phone call from the funeral director, asking us if we would agree to them transferring the burial from the Friday to Thursday because the staff at the cemetery were over-booked on the Friday. So, now my father's funeral was to take place on Thursday!

Heather shrieked, "There's the first bit of the message!"

I said, "I still want to see if the rest of what Lee said makes any sense until I can really accept it."

The funeral was due to leave from my brother's house, and I was standing at the top of a flight of steps outside so that I could nip back inside quickly to let my uncle know that it was time for him to start moving. My uncle had a disease that was very similar to dropsy, so he could only shuffle along slowly with the aid of a walking stick. When I saw the cortège come around the corner, I ran back inside to tell Uncle Alex to make a start. I told Heather that she had better come as well.

"Why?" she asked.

I just said, "Please come."

She followed me back outside and there on the passenger car behind the hearse was a large wreath in the shape of a fish!

When the cortège stopped outside of the flats, the funeral director - was an acquaintance of mine - said "Hello Gordon, everything all right?"

I asked him to swap the wreaths so that the one at the back could go onto the hearse.

"Oh, I can't do that mate," he replied, "That one is from the friends and neighbours in the street where your father lived."

I said, "He wants it there."

"Oh my gawd, are you one of them? Okay, I'll do it."

The wreaths were changed over - much to the chagrin of my other two brothers, although Jeff was happy about it. This now completed the message we had received on the Sunday evening, so we went off to the funeral. My Uncle Alex was intrigued as to what we were talking about and I had to explain it to him when we were in the car. He just laughed and said, "My mum used to tell me about things like that."

I was walking back to the car with the funeral director and discussing payment, when I commented to him that I was surprised that he had acceded to my request about moving the "fish" wreath to the hearse.

He replied, "Oh, that's simple. I didn't want to take the chance of upsetting anybody again." Then he went on to say, "Don't get me wrong; I don't understand what goes on with you people, but I had a similar request about a year ago and I refused. For a week, nothing went right in my business, and it wasn't until my son who works with me suddenly said to me, "Dad, none of these problems existed until we did Mrs X's funeral - shall we go and have a chat with her?"

When we saw Mrs X, she explained Spiritualism to us, and after we apologised to her things started to go right again. My wife works in the office, she couldn't understand why papers had gone missing and things that were normally fine were going wrong all through the week. The morning after seeing Mrs X, everything was back in its place and back to normal! When you asked me to change the wreaths over, I did so because I didn't want any more trouble."

I told him that Pop would not have liked it either, but that I did not think he would have made the funeral director's life difficult, but I thanked him for respecting my request. Once I arrived home, I had a very long think about these extraordinary events and came to the conclusion that I could no longer have any doubts about the survival of the soul or about working with Spirit.

*****

There is another story that is related to the previous one. After asking for the fish wreath to be placed on the front car, I went to have a word with the lady who had ordered the wreath. She turned out to be a neighbour who had lived in the flat beneath my father. Pop had been a friendly man he liked to help people out but using his hobby of clock and watch repairs for the benefit of others. On my father's death, the solicitor I had consulted suggested that I place a notice in the newspaper so that anyone who had given Pop something to repair could claim back their goods. Neighbours and friends had seen the notice in the local newspaper and enquired from another neighbour called Peggy as to where they should send flowers. Peggy realised that there would be quite a few who would want to do this, but that while some were reasonably well off, others were not. Peggy put a biscuit tin on the floor inside her front door and asked the neighbours to just put some money in the tin saying that she would get something on behalf of them all. The neighbours put everything from five-pound notes to a few pence into the tin.

Later that week, Peggy picked up the tin of money and decided to go to the nearby florist on the way to work, but when she got there it was closed. This made no sense whatsoever, as this florist had never been shut before. She decided to carry on her journey to work. When she reached her destination, she got off the bus, looked across the road and saw a florist. She had never even noticed the place before. Peggy and the florist totted up the money and then considered what to do with the amount. Peggy explained to the florist that she wanted something that was suitable as a tribute from neighbours and friends. The florist was halfway through the paperwork when he suddenly stopped writing and said, "You're not talking about Pop Smith in Furness Road are you?" Very surprised, Peggy answered that she was.

The florist said, "He can't be dead - he's my mate. We went fishing together only last Sunday." After a little more conversation they agreed that the florist should make up a wreath in the shape of a fish.

Apparently, the neighbours called Pop "the mad fisherman" due to his habit of getting up early to go fishing, so Frank, the florist, devised the wreath in the shape of a fish. He thought the friends and neighbours would appreciate it - and they most certainly did. Either Pop or Spirit was instrumental in Frank making that wreath in the shape of a fish.

CHAPTER SEVENTEEN

Another death and more confirmation

After Pop died, rather than paying occasional visits to my younger brother, Derek, who was in hospital, my brother Jeff and I devised a plan. We discovered that Pop used to visit the hospital at the same time every day, spending half an hour or more with Derek. On weekdays, my other two brothers went in to see Derek when they could but Jeff and I decided to pay regular weekend visits.

Derek had multiple sclerosis, and while he was still reasonably capable at this time, he couldn't speak much due to the constriction in his throat muscles. He could still play cards though and he loved cribbage, so we played cribbage with him on a Saturday and a Sunday until he could no longer do so. After visiting Derek, Jeff and I would go back to his house, have something to eat and then return to the hospital, staying until eight o'clock in the evening. We would then return on a Sunday afternoon and stay until Derek's tea arrived around at six o'clock.

During the year after Pop's death, Derek deteriorated quite drastically. He could no longer sit up unaided and he was lying in a cot propped up with pillows. He communicated by hand signals and blinks of his eyes, and it was marvellous for us to discover that we could communicate with our brother in that condition. We chatted to him and then Jeff and I would play cribbage while he just watched. The expressions on his face showed us that he enjoyed it. On one particular Saturday, my brother and I went to see him at around four o'clock, but when the time came to leave, I suddenly had a very strong feeling that I shouldn't go home. I didn't feel as though I was being "told" anything at the time, but I just did not want to leave. I told Jeff that I wouldn't come back to his house for a meal and that I wanted to stay. He replied that if I stayed, he would too.

A few minutes later, my brother Colin turned up and said that he intended to visit Derek the next day and that he wanted to know if there was anything Derek needed from him. Derek signalled to Colin that there was nothing. Colin then told us that he had picked this time as he thought that my brother Jeff and I would have gone for our meal. Jeff explained to him that under normal circumstances we would not have been there but that I had a kind of instinct about staying and that he was going along with it.

"Oh, his rubbish," Colin answered.

I said "Well, don't think about it Colin, I'm staying anyway."

Colin left while Jeff and I stayed. Five o'clock came and went and I was beginning to wonder if my instinct had been wrong. It was nearing half past five, when there was suddenly a movement in the bed. My brother Jeff still says that he saw nothing other than Derek closing his eyes, but I definitely saw Derek half sit up, look into the corner of the room, and as clear as a bell, say, "Okay Pop, I'm coming." Then I saw his body flop backwards onto the bed but I saw an image of him travelling up towards the corner of the room, so I said a prayer for him.

Jeff went to tell the hospital staff what had happened, and when I went out into the corridor, I saw a doctor and nurse pushing a resuscitation trolley. I immediately stood in front of it and told the doctor that she was not going to resuscitate my brother. The doctor said that she had to do so, but I still refused to allow it and I continued to block her path. I told her to forget her commitment to her job, and said that Derek was happier where he was and was better off. I said that she could not resuscitate him to continue a life where he needed to be looked after like a tiny baby. We argued for a while but I remained firmly stood in front of the trolley, refusing to allow her to move it any further. She then looked at her watch, said that it was now too late to resuscitate Derek, and said, "You will have to sign the release form for me."

I told her that it would not be a problem and that I would sign as many forms as she wanted. We went back to her office where she then telephoned for another doctor. The second doctor arrived and then started to berate me for preventing her staff from performing their duties. I retaliated by pointing out the state that Derek had been in. Thankfully, it was finally was resolved and I told the doctors that I would sign any release forms that they wanted just so long as they left Derek alone. I then instructed them to place him in a casket, put him in a freezer and contact Edinburgh.

The lady doctor said, "Oh yes, I'd forgotten about that."

Prior to him becoming too ill to talk, Derek had agreed to a request from a hospital in Edinburgh to donate his body for research into multiple sclerosis. My father had signed the consent form, but after he died Jeff and I signed it again. Derek's body was duly placed in a casket and placed into the mortuary refrigerator and it was arranged that his body would be put on the Edinburgh train at ten o'clock that night.

Once back at Jeff's home he commented, "We had better ring Colin and let him know that there is no point in his going in to see Derek tomorrow." Upon being given the information, Colin had the audacity to tell Jeff to pass on the message that he wanted absolutely nothing more to do with me from that day forward because I had somehow organised it!

Jeff and I arranged a memorial service with the President of my Church in Surbiton for around a fortnight later. I told the family, but Colin again said that I had organised everything before Derek had died because, as he said, "it was impossible to have a memorial service in under six weeks - that was Church law".

Well, it might have been his church law (Colin is a Roman Catholic) but it is not the law at our Spiritualist church. Colin

arranged a second memorial service at his Church and told me
that I would not be welcome to attend and that the priest would
not allow me in. Jeff told him that we both would be there.

In the event, both my younger brothers, Colin and Michael,
came to the memorial service at the Spiritualist church, and they
went away saying that they were going to think about everything
that had taken place. There was no clairvoyant demonstration
during the service but it had been taken by a medium.

Jeff and I arrived at the Catholic Church for the second
memorial service, and as I walked to the lychgate, the priest asked
who I was. When I asked him why, he said that he just wanted to
know which side of the Church to place me as the family was to
be seated on one side and friends on the other.

I said, "I'm Gordon, Derek's brother."

"Oh, you're the eldest brother?"

I nodded.

"You're the medium?" he asked.

"Yes," I replied.

"Good, I want to talk to you after the service, if you don't
mind. Can I have ten minutes?"

When the service was over, I was somewhat bemused. It is
not often that I see clairvoyantly, but on that day I not only saw
my brother on the altar platform but also two of my Spiritual
Guides, one of whom is a Roman Catholic Archbishop who I
could see in full regalia. I also saw members of my family who
had passed over, including Pop, my mother and my sister.
Standing between my mother and father was my Native American
healing Guide, who is called Firehawk, and nearby I could see
Merlin, who is my Guide when I give readings. They were
bunched together behind the priest who was taking the service,
and they knew I could see them because they were waving to me!
I was given a real gift that day.

At the end of the service, the two priests came up to me and
asked me to go with them to the sanctuary. I followed them and
they questioned me very intelligently about my beliefs and about

Spiritualism. They were particularly interested in the laying on of hands, because they told me that this had been part of the Catholic faith until 1840. The Pope of the day banned it in 1888 due to adverse publicity relating to the Fox sisters.* My brother Colin was curious as to why I had been invited to talk with the priests, and when he quizzed Jeff, Heather and my other brother they all suggested that he should ask me. He still refused to speak to me, so I don't know to this day if anyone explained anything to him.

* The Spiritualist movement began in 1848 in a house in Hydesville in New York State in the USA where Leah, Margeretta and Kate Fox lived. The house was beset by paranormal events, such as ghosts and unexplained knocking, and the parents of the Fox sisters felt that a disturbed spirit was to blame. Margeretta and Kate began communicating with spirits - to the point where they eventually became celebrity figures. However, in 1888 the sisters were forced to admit that they had been faking their communications.

CHAPTER EIGHTEEN

The British Astrological and Psychic Society

In 1975, BAPS was invited to provide readers for the then extremely exciting Mind Body and Spirit Festival, which was being held at Olympia in Kensington. After the first few years, this festival moved to the Royal Horticultural Halls near Victoria, where it has been ever since. BAPS has mounted a stand at the festival every year since the beginning. The festival is no longer as exciting as it was in those heady days in the 1970s when the whole spiritual, alternative, green and hippy ideas were taking off, but it is still an important event for those who are interested in spiritual matters. I didn't actually give readings at this first festival; I just helped out on reception. I did take a table and give readings at the second festival and I have worked at every one since.* I would like to think that I have been doing people some good during that time. This was the main festival of its kind during the year, but there were (and still are) others.

* The Festival of Mind, Body and Spirit at the Royal Horticultural Halls in Victoria in London that was held in May 2002 was Gordon's final public appearance before his passing. He had attended this particular festival for twenty-six years without fail.

In the early years, the President of BAPS was a lady who unfortunately wanted to be in control of everything, despite the fact that we had a committee. One day, a lady approached my table, laid her ticket down and began to remove her coat. Each client would give the reader a ticket, which was matched with the bookings on the form at the reception table, and it was this that allowed the readers to be paid a proportion of what the client paid to have their reading

As the woman released one shoulder from her coat, suddenly her "double" appeared alongside her. As I have said before, I very rarely see clairvoyantly, but now and again Spirit makes it possible, and it happened again on this particular occasion.

I asked her, "Do you have a sister in Spirit?"

She replied, "No, but my father tells me that I am the image of my mother at the same age."

I asked if her mother was in Spirit and she confirmed she was. I then said, "Then your mother is standing beside you, because I am seeing your double. She says that you made your mind up last night and she is asking you why you are here?"

The lady said, "Oh, thank you very much, that was all I wanted to know."

With that, she put her coat back on, dropped the ticket on my table and left with a smile on her face. The receptionist who we had at the time followed the lady and spoke to her, because she was concerned that this client might have been short-changed. The festival organiser, who was also the President of the Society, walked up to my table and grabbed my ticket. She told me that I would not be paid for the reading because I had once again upset someone. To my knowledge there had never been any previous complaints about me.

I just sat and looked at her and didn't say a word, because I felt very calm within myself and felt no need to respond. I put this down to Spirit, as I do not normally stay so calm when I am being spoken to in such an offensive manner. While this scolding went on, a thought entered my head, and it was:

"If someone 'attacks' you in a derogatory manner and it is not warranted, if you stay still and quiet, then the problem goes back onto the person who is doing the attacking."

The President took the ticket away and left my table.

A lady sitting at the next table to mine had been forced to discontinue her reading because of this incident. She looked at me and said, "Gordon, you're not going to take that, are you? I know what happened because I saw it."

I answered, "Love, it doesn't worry me, it won't hurt me." She replied, "Well, I wouldn't take it."

I said, "No, but Spirit prevented me from speaking out and I don't know why."

About an hour later, the reason became obvious. The receptionist, who had followed the lady and spoken to her, came to my table and said, "By the way Gordon, I've retrieved your ticket from the bin so here it is. That lady was extremely pleased. She told me that you had given her exactly what she had come in to find out about and that she just wanted the confirmation that you gave her."

I was grateful to her and I thanked her for letting me know.

The receptionist continued, "And I have already told the President what I have just told you."

I asked her what answer she had been given.

She said, "That she wasn't putting up with any more and that she was going to resign if anything else happened."

A little later on I became aware of a dispute at the reception area and a colleague of mine came up to me and said, "Gordon, do you realise that that young man on reception is using bad language to the clients?"

I was astonished and said; "You're joking."

He said, "No I'm not, people are complaining about it." Unfortunately, the young man on reception happened to be the President's son. When challenged, the President denied that her son would ever speak in this way, but the people involved insisted that he had. She then became extremely agitated and suddenly announced that she was resigning. Nobody said a word.

When we started to pack up at the end of the day, she turned to me and said, "Gordon, this is all your fault!"

I did not know what she meant and asked, "What is?"

She answered, "I'm resigning and nobody has opposed my decision."

I said, " Love, it's your choice."

It was only after the acceptance of her resignation that the Society returned to a normal footing. The Vice-President took over, and at the following committee meeting, the work that the previous President had hugged to herself was allocated out to various members, and this continues to be the case.

This President had taken most of the work of the Society upon herself and she had made herself ill because of it. She was reluctant to share the work, and eventually it had all become too much for her to cope with. I feel that this episode had been Spirit's way of moving her on, as she is now working extremely well elsewhere.

*****

BAPS has a strict vetting procedure that takes place before a Reader is allowed to become a consultant. Although I had used the Dakini cards for quite some time, I could not use them with BAPS at festivals because there was nobody to check whether I was using them correctly. BAPS has rules, which are the same for members of the committee as they are for newcomers, and one major one is that no person can work on a BAPS stand at a festival unless they have been vetted and awarded the BAPS Certificate of Competence.

*****

One day I was attending a festival in Cardiff when I saw a gentleman enter the hall. I thought he looked rather pretentious, as he was dressed in a long leather coat that was covered in symbols, his hair was long and braided at the back and he walked with a staff. To my surprise he walked over to my table, sat down and asked for a reading. I was using the Rider-Waite deck Tarot cards at the time but he specifically asked for the Dakini cards. After gaining permission from the President at that time, I did this for him, after which he proclaimed that he was satisfied with the reading.

At the next committee meeting of BAPS, I was told that I had passed my vetting and had gained my Certificate for the Dakini cards! It turned out that the man who had come to my table in Cardiff was called Arturo, and he had lived in the east. He was actually an Australian by birth but had spent many years in the Orient, and had actually helped to design the Dakini cards. My colleague had known this and had asked Arturo if he would examine me for them. Arturo subsequently contacted my colleague with a written report to the effect that he was very satisfied with the way in which I had used the Dakini cards and that I had been accurate with my reading. A very unusual vetting!

CHAPTER NINETEEN

The psychic boy, a short trip to the "other side" and other stories

I was still working as an engineer during the day. One day, I arrived home from work when the landlady popped in to see me. She said to me, "In case you notice your room has been disturbed, it is because you had a visitor today. You'll be moving out in about six weeks. Someone from the Council came today and looked round your room, and they seemed satisfied with the condition of it."

Five weeks later, I received a letter offering me Council accommodation at a flat, which had the number thirteen. I went to view it and discovered that it was a nice airy flat, so I went to the Council office and told them that I would take it. The lady I saw there said, "Before you sign the forms, I have to tell you that you can't have the number changed!" I told her that the number didn't bother me. She then told me that the flat had previously been offered to three other people, and each one of them had asked for the number to be changed as they thought the number thirteen would be unlucky.

There were two free local papers that used to be delivered in that area, but only one ever came through my letterbox. The other was invariably dropped on the floor by the entrance to the corridor that I lived on. One Christmas I happened to be around when the lads who delivered the papers came around, and I stopped them, as I wanted to give them a Christmas "box". As usual, one of the papers was lying on the floor in the corridor. I asked the paperboy who actually put one of the papers through my door why the other boy always threw his paper on the floor just inside the door. He said that he would ask, and then he returned bringing a lad of about twelve or thirteen with him, but the other boy remained standing outside the door to the main corridor. I walked out and asked him why he would not put the paper through my door. He told me that he could not walk down the corridor. He said to me, "When I walk in through this door, I get a funny feeling and I just can't go any further."

I thought to myself "Here is somebody who is going to be working in a similar vein to me later in life."

I told him I understood but said, "Next time, try."

He told me that in addition to feeling uncomfortable on my corridor, he did not like the number thirteen. I told him that the number had nothing to do with anything and repeated what I had said to him. I then asked the boy what was making him feel uncomfortable, and he said that it was as he moved into the corridor that he felt he had to behave well. I told him not to worry about it and that he would learn why later on in life. It took two or three weeks before my paper finally appeared through my front door but I never discovered whether he actually did it himself or whether the other paperboy did it for him.

*****

My life continued with my healing, sitting in circles from time to time and working with Spirit. One day, I received an invitation to inaugurate a Church in Dublin. The people there asked me to bring along a colleague, as they also wanted me to perform healing demonstrations. They asked me if I had a colleague who was a clairvoyant and who would be willing to come along with me, who could take the opening service on the Sunday. At that time I had a working partner who was called Lynne. Lynne and I attended nation-wide demonstrations together as well as some shows, but these were mainly confined to the area in and around London. I asked her if she would accompany me to inaugurate the church in Dublin, and she said that she would have to ask her husband. This presented a problem because her husband considered that what we did was "a load of rubbish", so she was not sure if he would agree.

This situation is amazingly common among couples where one works in the Spiritual movement and the other doesn't. Perhaps the sceptical partner has been "chosen" to keep the spiritualist's feet on the ground. Personally, I feel that these partners must have some belief or they would not let their partner work at all, but they usually spend a fair bit of time putting the spiritual partner down. Lynne thought the best way to approach her husband was to invite me to dinner.

After dinner, Lynne turned to Tom and told him that she had been asked to help inaugurate a new Church in Dublin and to do some demonstrations, and she asked if he would be happy for her to do this. He replied that he would have to think about it and then asked when it was. Lynne told him that it was to occur in four week's time. He asked me how long he could take in order to make his mind up, and I replied that we really only had until the weekend, as I had to confirm the flight bookings. The remainder of the evening went very well.

As I was leaving, Tom came up to me to say goodnight and then asked, "Are you going to Dublin?"

"Yes. In fact, I was the one who received the invitation and I was asked if I could take a clairvoyant with me, which is why I had asked Lynne to accompany me."

He said that he had no objection to Lynne accompanying me. Relieved, I thanked him and left.

Two days later, I received a telephone call from Lynne to tell me that Tom had changed his mind but to leave it with her for a few days.

I then came down with a severe cold. I spent a couple of days indoors; during which time I received a phone call from the airline asking for confirmation on the tickets to Dublin. I thought that I had better go and see Tom and Lynne despite the fact that my cold appeared to have turned into flu. I turned up at Tom and Lynne's home, walked in and then immediately passed out! Had this happened while I was at home, I would have had no way of contacting my doctor. Apparently, while I was unconscious, I turned a strange colour and Tom was very concerned. His doctor only lived four doors away from them, so Tom went and banged on his door and asked him to come and see me. As he came in, I felt myself entering "the other side", but I came back a few minutes later to find the doctor taking a needle out of my side.

On this short journey to "other side", I had a lovely conversation with my father and my sister. I also saw Derek in the distance in running clothes. He had always wanted to be a runner when he was here on earth, but could never do this due to him being an invalid. I was quite a distance away from my father, so I walked towards him. I could hear him perfectly and apparently he could also hear me.

As I stepped towards him he said, "No Son, you've got work to do."

It was at this point that I came to, with the doctor removing a needle from my chest. I realised where I had been and that it was truly wonderful. I don't have any intentions of getting there ahead of time but I am looking forward to going back!

*****

Tom finally gave his permission for Lynne to accompany me to Dublin, although I spent the next two days camping out on his settee before being sent to hospital for examination. One evening when it was nice and quiet in the hospital, I had one of my "meditation moments" and Spirit came nearby. I told Spirit that I didn't actually realise that I was on the other side while I was over there, and I only woke up to what had happened after I returned. I also didn't know exactly where I was on the other side or in which realm or area. To me, moving to the other side had been like continuing a conversation with my father after an interruption, but I had no recollection of when the conversation had started. I asked Spirit why this was.

Spirit told me that it is easier for Spiritualists to cope with the move because we know what it will be like. We realise that we go from one land to another and one country to another, but that once we have crossed the borders we cannot return, except via a medium. I told them I understood that. Spirit then asked me to consider those who didn't believe that there is another life after this one. Did I not think that they would panic when they arrived? That is why family or friends always come to greet them. That made sense to me and I asked if they did this with everybody. They told me that they did. I then asked how was it that my father was able to come back to prove a point only three days after his passing. Spirit explained that when a person arrives at the other side, he or she discovers that the vibrations of time and space are much faster than those that we experience on earth, and that my father had become aware of this very quickly. He had realised that all I had been telling him had been true and he had explained to Spirit that he had to come back for a while in order to prove this to me. They had allowed him to come back to prove his point on the transmigration of the soul because it was necessary, but that this doesn't often happen. Most people are allowed time to become aware of where they are and what has happened to them and this could take several days by our earth time. The world on the other side has no conception of time as we know it. Usually those who pass over are quite relaxed about what has happened to them, and it is only those who are left behind who are upset.

As soon as I recovered, I left hospital, telephoned the airline and was told that I wasn't too late to confirm the booking, so I sent off the money for the ticket and Lynne and I went to Ireland for the weekend.

*****

We inaugurated the Church and I conducted a demonstration on the Saturday morning at a nearby hall. There were people who wanted healing so I carried on, finally finishing half an hour before Lynne's demonstration was due to start at seven in the evening! I had a quick cup of coffee and a snack before it was time to start the evening demonstration. This went down very well, but there were still people asking to experience the healing. It ended up with Lynne on the platform giving her clairvoyant demonstration and me in a corner behind a screen giving healing. The evening was a huge success.

Lynne and I returned to the place that we were staying in, which was owned by a lady called Patricia, who was also a member of the Church. It turned out that Patricia and her sister, Madeline, had been nuns. Lynne was able to regress to the past, so she knew that Madeline had been a pregnant nun in the monastery! We all laughed about it, including Pat's and her sister's husband - and although Madeline was not too happy about it, she accepted the information.

The following morning at around ten o'clock, Pat's doorbell started ringing with people calling to see either Lynne or me for healing. One or two from the previous day had come back because they had enjoyed it so much. Before we knew it, about twenty people had turned up and it was one o'clock before Pat sent them away and told them to come back to the Church in the evening. Lynne and I had the afternoon to ourselves and Pat's husband, Sean, took us out to see the area. When we arrived at the airport on Monday morning, the staff there told us that we might not be able to fly because the mechanics that usually worked on the aeroplanes were on strike. Suddenly, the strike was called off. The flight manager was amazed at this because to his knowledge, no negotiations had taken place. Apparently the mechanics just decided to go back to work. My friends in Dublin sent me a newspaper carrying a very nice article about Lynne and myself.

The events surrounding my collapse just prior to going to Ireland had apparently influenced Lynne's Tom quite considerably, so he began to ask questions and talk about what we did. Thus, it proves that some good came out of that.

*****

One day, soon after this event, quite out of the blue Lynne said that she had decided that she did not want to do this work any more. She promptly left, telling me that she did not want to hear from me or see me again! I returned to my flat totally confused.

Almost a month later, I bumped into Audrey, who was Lynne's best friend. Audrey asked me if I had seen anything of Lynne and I said that I hadn't. I told her about Lynne's peculiar behaviour the previous month and Audrey nodded her head. I asked her if she knew something about it. Audrey told me that Lynne and Tom's marriage was in tatters - as was hers. I told her I was sorry to hear about that and asked if there was anything I could do to help. She said there wasn't and that she and her husband were attempting to sort things out for themselves. Audrey relayed to me that she worked in the afternoons, but that a month earlier she had felt unwell and her boss had sent her home. When she arrived home she saw her husband's car outside and wondered why he was home so early. When she went inside, she caught her husband, Bill, in bed with Lynne!

Tom told Lynne that she was to move into a separate bedroom and they would only be staying together for the sake of the children. He also forbade her to do any more Spiritual work. I said that I was very sorry to hear of this and that I hoped it worked out for them. I asked Audrey what was happening with her, and she said that she was going to try and patch things up with her husband. I have not seen Audrey or Bill from that day to this, and when I made enquiries I discovered that they had moved. I felt that it was a shame as they were a lovely couple.

Unfortunately, this is just part of life and it proves that, regardless of our good work with Spirit, at the end of the day, we are still human beings, we make mistakes and have to move on.

*****

Nowadays, my hands are twisted due to arthritis, they ache at times and I am no longer capable of doing much writing or typing. However, when I sit down at a festival and hand a deck of cards to a client to shuffle, they hand them back to me and I turn the cards and talk, my hands are free of pain. Everything works fine then, but as soon as I am finished the pain returns. I always thank Spirit for allowing me to continue doing my work.

CHAPTER TWENTY

A brief incursion into show business

There is a saying that when one door closes another door opens...

One evening Russell Grant telephoned me and asked if I could arrange to take a day off work and pick him up to take him somewhere by car. It turned out that he wanted to go to Southend. We went to a house where a friend of Russell's lived, but when we got there, the friend's mother told us that he was at a local Church hall rehearsing a play. I asked Russell what was going on but he told me to just to take him to meet his friend. Russell's friend, Mr Bridge, was pleased to see us and asked us to sit and wait while he finished rehearsing a young group of teenagers who were dancing and acting.

Russell spoke to his friend, saying, "This is the man I brought for you to see in connection with the question you asked me the other night. He knows more about it than I do."

I said, "Will somebody please explain to me what's going on?"

Mr Bridge then told me he was an actor/manager and that he wanted to put on psychic shows in a theatre, but that he wanted to know how to do it. I told him that I would tell him as much as I knew and that I knew people who could give him more information. He then invited us to lunch. He had been introduced to me as Mr Alexander Bridge.

During the lunch he asked me if I would work with him, after which we returned to the Church hall because he needed to continue with the rehearsals. While in the car, Mr Bridge said, "Right, from now on, you call me Peter."

Russell and I stopped off on the way back for a coffee and while we were having our refreshments, Russell gave me a quizzical look. I asked him if anything was wrong and he just said that he was trying to work something out. He said that he had known Mr Bridge since they had been in drama school together, but that people were only able to call him "Peter" with his permission, and usually only after several months of his knowing them. The fact that he had told me to call him Peter after a couple of hour's acquaintance was strange.

Two or three weeks later, I received a phone call from Peter asking if I could meet him in Southend. Peter had decided to put on his first Psychic Show in the Gray's Theatre and he needed to contact people who would appear in the show. We made a few phone calls there and then and obtained a few promises. After this, he put his head on one side and commented that we had made up to a dozen phone calls but that I hadn't referred to a diary, but that I had simply drawn the numbers out of my head. I told him that this was just something that I could do because that once I have seen a telephone number, I could always remember it.

I attended the first show as a healer. The show was a success and we also had a few visitors from the press due to Peter being quite well known in the theatre profession. Peter and I took to each other from the start, and our friendship grew quickly. Peter's friends could not understand our friendship at all, partly because I was not a member of the theatre profession and also because I was heterosexual while Peter was gay. This was irrelevant to us because we just accepted each other for who we were and we enjoyed our friendship.

We put on several more successful shows in the Essex area and then another at the Town Hall in Greenwich. While we were there, a lady turned up and said that she wanted to present leaflets for a show that she was putting on in a few weeks' time in the same area. Peter told her that she had a bit of a cheek, but he appeared to like her. When speaking with her, he discovered that not only was she a medium, but also a numerologist. That was a divination that he did not have among his group, so Peter suggested that she take a table at our show. She was reasonably popular because she could read cards and she also added clairvoyance to her numerology. (Numerology being the study of numbers and how they can affect your life).

After the show, Peter asked her if she would like to join up with us. She said that she would, and Peter told her that the next show was due to be held in Stevenage. She seemed a bit upset about this and when Peter asked her why, she explained that she could not use public transport and she could not drive.

Peter turned to me and asked if I would mind taking her. I said that I would be happy to do so, and this was the start of a partnership between Carla and me. It is not essential to have a partner when you work at such shows, but it is nice to have one. It is good to have someone to be with and to be able to chat over a meal in the evenings ,as well as having a bit of company to travel with. Another more practical reason is that in many of these shows, the table that one rents is too large and expensive for one person, so two people usually join forces.

Carla continued to do her own shows as well as attending some with me, and we found working alongside each other comfortable - and this is not always easy when you are working with spirit.

One day, Carla asked me if I could get off work early to meet her at her house at half past four. When I arrived, Carla told me her husband was due home shortly but asked me to say nothing to him. I was somewhat puzzled by this. Carla's husband duly arrived home, saw me and stopped dead in his tracks.

He looked at me and asked, "Are you Gordon?" He turned to Carla and said, "For once, you were telling the truth." He then added, "All right Carla, I won't make any more comments about you going out on these shows." Then he turned to me and apologised.

Apparently, although Carla had told him that I was an older man and that we just worked together, her husband had not believed her. He thought she had a new boyfriend!

I mentally said to Spirit, "You do get me into some scrapes, don't you? First there was Lynne and Tom and now it's Carla and Ian."

Carla and I travelled around the country to various shows, and despite my hours of work being erratic, we always made it to the shows. I would say to Spirit, "If I'm meant to be there, please make sure I am", and it invariably turned out that I was.

*****

An old friend of mine called George Dale who I had worked with in a group in West Moseley decided that since his retirement, he wanted to move to be nearer to his children. He had worked as a pharmacist and had been in business all of his life in that particular field. He was a true chemist, to the extent that he had very little in the way of manufactured goods in his shop as he used to make up medicines and ointments himself. We shared a hobby of painting and we used to spend time in a little shed in his garden, which he called his "studio".

One evening while we were happily painting, George said, "You have no ties and I am planning to move to Grimsby and I want to open a shop selling spiritual goods. I would like you to be the medium in the back giving readings. Would you like that?"

Once the arrangements were made, I told Carla that I would be moving away, but anyway our arrangement seemed to be coming to an end of its own accord. We had a weekend show booked at Bletchley and we intended to take a pupil of Carla's along to work with us. I must admit that I was not a hundred per cent certain of his capabilities - but the pupil, whose name was Alan, came with us. It proved to be quite a successful show, but when we were breaking down the stand, Carla suddenly said that she needed to visit the ladies room. Alan turned to me to thank me for the opportunity of allowing him to attend the weekend show. I said I was pleased that he had enjoyed it and that I hoped to see him with us again some time. Alan then said, "Oh, you'll see me again, but not with yourself and Carla!"

I asked him what he meant by that, and he said that Carla had wanted to tell me that they were now a partnership and that she would not be working with me any more. I was taken aback. I didn't show my feelings, but I was actually very hurt by this revelation, because Carla had not told me herself. That was the end of our partnership, but the start of a new life for Carla and Alan, because shortly after that, they broke up their respective marriages and moved in with each other.

CHAPTER TWENTY-ONE

The medium, the dog and the canary

I was now a year away from my retirement from work. One day I walked into the office to find my usually happy and pleasant boss with a very long face. I asked him what had happened and he said, "Sorry mate, we're out of work. The receivers walked in at twelve o'clock and we finish at four... we are all redundant. You must take your car home, take your personal belongings out and bring it back here by four o'clock, and a mini-bus will be taking us all home.

I did as I was asked, all the while thinking to myself, "Where was I going to get another job now?"

On the Monday morning I went to my bank to tell them what had happened, only to be told I was in the red. I said that this couldn't be possible, as I was always very careful with my money. The Assistant Manager then told me that I had not been paid any salary for seven weeks. I had been totally unaware of this and had been spending my money as usual. I had been getting my pay slips from the office so it hadn't occurred to me that they weren't actually paying me. The Assistant Manager told me not to worry and said that he had already given some thought to the problem. He asked me for my chequebook and bank guarantee card together with any credit cards I held. I gave them to him and he then disappeared for about twenty minutes. He then handed me a new chequebook and card and he told me that he had placed £250 into my account. He explained that he had sealed my account and he told me to be careful until the problem was sorted out, but that if I needed more than this, I was to let him know.

I went straight to the Job Centre and "signed on". They told me that I would not receive any money for six weeks. I explained the situation to the clerk, but his only response was to say, "That's your problem!"

A man who was walking behind the clerk who I was talking with stopped and asked him what the problem was. The clerk relayed to him everything I had told him and the gentleman said, "No, it isn't his problem. We have a special supplementary fund for people in this type of situation, don't you know about it?"

The clerk said, "Oh yes, I know about it but I didn't think he would be eligible."

The gentleman asked for all my paperwork and requested that I should follow him. We went to another desk and he went through the paperwork again. He told me that I would receive the minimum payment for six weeks and that when my unemployment payments came through, they would deduct a little per week as repayment for this supplementary help. I said I was happy with that and I left. When I arrived home, I pondered about my position. I didn't want the only work the Job Centre could offer me, which was pushing trolleys around a supermarket, so I returned to the Bank and asked to speak to someone about self-employment. Two days later, an ex-colleague from work telephoned me and told me that his brother was going to work in Dubai and that he had a car to sell. It was a four-year-old Honda Accord and he said that I could have it for £1,000 if I could find the money by Friday.

I thought, "Somebody upstairs is working for me."

It occurred to me that if I did go into business for myself I would need a car, so I said yes and then went back to the bank and explained the situation to the Assistant Manager. I told him that the firm's customers would not have anyone to carry out their repairs now that the company had gone into liquidation. I said that I could advertise for additional work, but either way I would need a car. I then told him about the offer that I had received. He asked me to give him ten minutes and disappeared. He then came back and told me that the car was worth far more than that I had been asked to pay and said that he would lend me the £1,000. I gratefully thanked him and went to the teller's desk ten minutes later to collect the money. Friday morning, I went to Leatherhead and collected the car.

I heard afterwards from a couple of my neighbours that they had tried to obtain a bank loan, but had been turned down because they were told that they were too old, and they were younger than me! I put it all down to the fact that Spirit was giving me a helping hand.

I canvassed all my old customers and some engaged me to do some work. It was slow at first and I did get into a bit of debt, but I thought I could get out of it and anyway, I was doing something that I enjoyed. Unfortunately, the reality was that the work began to die away. I discovered the customers thought I was too old and they gave the larger, heavier jobs to younger engineers. Yet again, I found myself having to think about what to do next.

I continued to work on my own until George Dale phoned to tell me that he was looking for a shop in Grimsby. George's idea was to sell spiritual accessories and for me to contribute to the business by selling crystals, giving readings when requested and generally helping out in the shop.

I placed my furniture into storage and moved to Grimsby. We found a shop that was suitable and organised the renovations that were needed. In the meantime, I searched for accommodation and stayed in a bed and breakfast until finding a flat via the local Council. At last, the day arrived when we were due to collect the keys to open the shop. Then I got a message that George had suffered a fatal heart attack - so no shop! I did not have sufficient funds to continue the venture on my own and George's family had no interest in it, but I had my flat and I eventually managed to find work as a private taxi driver.

In the meantime, I was continuing with my Spiritual work. Unfortunately, I then became ill and it took a long time before the doctors could figure out what was wrong. Six weeks later, I received an invitation to look at some sheltered accommodation in Basildon, so I decided to make the move back down south.

When I visited the flat in Basildon, I realised someone who I had previously worked with at festivals lived in the same block of flats. The gentleman and his wife and invited me to stay with them for a couple of days while inspecting the flat. When I got back to Grimsby I received a letter on a Monday morning informing me that removers would be arriving on the Friday and that I was to have everything ready. I had four days in which to pack.

On moving back to Basildon I was admitted to hospital - ostensibly for a check-up, but I ended up staying for five and a half weeks. It appeared that there had been a problem with my medication, but once that was sorted out, along with the rest in hospital, I was soon the road to recovery. I even worked at the 1996 Mind Body and Spirit Festival, and I have never missed one since. It appeared that Spirit wanted me to continue with this work.

*****

For the last twelve years, I have been assisting a lady called Pat Dickie with Psychic Seminars that she holds in Bournemouth every year. This all began when Pat telephoned me saying that she had an idea that she wanted to put to me, which was to advertise for people who would wish to attend a specific venue in order to learn more about psychic work. Her intention was to hire a hotel for a week so that those who wished to attend could have bed and board included in the price. She asked me what my feelings were about it and what I would want as payment for teaching about Spirit. We agreed that just my expenses would be covered. I told her that it was likely that various colleagues of mine would agree to attend on the same basis. Pat asked me to phone around to see how my colleagues would feel about the idea of working for expenses only. I received a good response from the likes of Sheila

McGuirk, Les Brown and a few others. In the meantime, Pat made enquiries about venues.

The first Psychic Seminar was held at a holiday camp. We gave lectures, demonstrations and talks, all of which were very well received. When we held a "post-mortem" afterwards as to whether we were going to do it again, somebody came up with the comment that we had been extremely lucky with the weather. Had it been bad weather, we would have had to pay for mud to be cleared from the conference rooms. The camp had let Pat have the rooms cheaply because she held the seminar during a quiet time of the year but with very few staff available, and if they had needed to hire cleaners, this would have been an extra expense for us. We realised that we needed to find a venue that was more suited to inclement weather. Pat looked for a hotel in Bournemouth, found one that was suitable and we have been holding the seminars at the same venue ever since. Each year, the number of people attending has increased. Some are regulars but there are also many new faces. We have had some really wonderful experiences at these Seminars, but there is one in particular that sticks out in my mind.

I act as the master of ceremonies for the stage demonstrations that are held in the evenings. We had planned a long demonstration on this particular evening, with two mediums working on the stage, including Pat if needed. The first medium began to work but she sat down again after a couple of messages, saying that the atmosphere was a bit heavy. It was true; the atmosphere was a bit heavy.

The second Medium stood up and said, "Look here Spirit, I'm fed up with giving messages from auntie this or uncle that, can I have something different please?"

She then started to chuckle because, walking down the centre aisle between where the audience were sitting, she said that she could see a large black shaggy dog which stopped at a lady who was seated at the end of a row. The "spirit dog" sat down. She then noticed that the dog had a canary on its head, and that the canary that was singing. She described all of this to the audience and people started laughing. This was all well and good, but the lady who the dog had chosen to sit beside could not relate to it, despite being able to accept everything else that the medium had told her.

The medium kept coming back to the dog, saying to the lady, "The dog hasn't moved. It is still sitting at the side of you and it is still looking up at you as if to say, 'Please recognise me'." The lady shook her head and said that she still did not understand.

While all of this was taking place, I had noticed that eight people who had been sitting the back of the room had walked out. Further messages were then given to others and the demonstrations ended with humour and laughter, both from the audience and from Spirit. Afterwards, we retired to the bar in the hotel as for once I didn't have to drive anywhere so I took advantage of the opportunity to have a drink. Pat asked me if I had noticed the people who had left. She then told me that they had asked for their money back.

I said, "You're joking - it's only the second day. Why?"

Pat replied, "They said it was because we are treating Spirit in a frivolous manner because we have been laughing." Pat told me that, according to them, Spirit is very serious and must be taken very seriously.

I said, "They ought to hear what my "friend" says to me now and again. What are you going to do?"

"I told them that they have paid for the week and that they can use the remainder of the time as a holiday if they wish but I will not refund them. Anyway, what did you think about the story of the dog?"

"I thought it was a nice one," I replied.

"Yes, so did I."

The next morning after breakfast, I was in the hall getting ready to conduct a workshop. The "lady with the dog" from the previous evening's demonstration came up to me and asked if she could have a word with me.

She told me that her husband would have nothing whatsoever to do with her Spiritual beliefs. She said that she saved up all year to come to the seminar and that her husband would only allow this on the proviso that she telephoned him every night. On that evening she phoned him and decided that, despite his lack of interest in the proceedings, she would tell him the funny story about the medium, the dog and the canary. Apparently the phone went silent for such a long time that she thought he had hung up on her, so she said that if he wasn't going to talk to her she would go off to bed. She said that her husband spluttered and asked her to tell him again what she'd said about the dog and the canary, so she repeated it - and then he astonished her by telling her the following story.

Andy said, "I don't know what to say. I never tell the story about the dog and the canary to anybody because it is embarrassing. The only time I ever mentioned it was when I was at school and I was ridiculed and called a liar so I never mentioned it again. My parents never mentioned it either for the same reasons. Nobody believed that a canary would actually sit on a dog's head or that a dog would allow a canary to sit on its head, but our dog did, and he used to enjoy it. He would walk around the house with the canary on his head and the canary would be singing quite happily."

Then he astonished his wife by asking her to book him in for the following year. Spirit gained a convert, but the way I like to think of it is that Spirit made it easier for this lady to attend the seminars without feeling guilty due to her husband's disapproval. Spirit will work in this way at times to make the pathway easier for people to go forward.

Regarding the eight people who walked out from the demonstration, I had a chat with one of them later and he told me that they all belonged to the same Church in Wales and had come to the seminar as a group. He asked me if I would approach Pat again on their behalf to ask her to refund them. I told them that I would not do this. He turned to me and said, "So you're as bad as everybody else. You don't take Spirit seriously either."

With that, we sat down and had quite a long conversation. I explained that I did, indeed, take Spirit very seriously. I also pointed out that when we go into the world of Spirit, we don't change our colour, our attitudes or our personality - at least, not at first. I also explained that there is bound to be aggravation, laughter, humour and all aspects of the personality that existed here on earth. Eventually he and his friends had to accept that sometimes there would be humour. I think he may have understood what I was trying to tell him but, sadly, he and his friends didn't attend any further demonstrations, although they did stay for the remainder of the week.

*****

A lady, who I knew, called Lorraine Hall, turned up at the seminar that same year. Lorraine was a good card reader and medium. I had tried to coax her to work at the seminar but she refused through fear of letting herself down. This particular year, however, Spirit took a hand.

It was my morning for conducting a workshop on the Tarot but while I was eating my breakfast, the top plate of my dentures suddenly broke. I was in a bit of a panic about this and went to the hotel reception for help and they kindly phoned round to find a laboratory that would repair my teeth quickly for me. While all of this was taking place, I asked Lorraine if she would act as my substitute and start the workshop off for me, as it was now impossible for me to do. Very reluctantly, she agreed. I assured her it would only be until I could get my teeth repaired and that I would return as soon as I could. I then went to the laboratory, leaving Lorraine shaking like a leaf at the prospect of having to take the workshop. When I reached the laboratory, they found it incredible that I had broken my plate simply by eating toast. They said it would have been more believable if I had been chewing on a bone! They quickly repaired my teeth and I was able to return to the hotel, arriving toward the end of the workshop. When I walked into the hotel, I saw Pat hiding behind the door of the workshop area.

Curious, I asked her if everything was all right and she replied, "Absolutely. You were right, she is good."

I said, "Well, I think Spirit had something to do with this, don't you?"

"Yes, I do," she replied.

I walked into the workshop, watched for a while and soon realised that Lorraine was in her element. She produced an excellent workshop by getting everyone working together in groups, so there was nothing for me to do. I laughed afterwards when Lorraine said how quickly the time had passed, because it had been a two-hour workshop. She was pleased at how it had turned out and said that she had even surprised herself, as she had not realised her own expertise. During the following two years, Lorraine took the workshops and there was no longer any need for me to participate.

This is an example of Spirit knowing what we can do, despite our own trepidation. Sometimes Spirit will devise a plan to persuade a person to do something that they fear. Spirit will not force it on anyone, and after all, Lorraine did not have to take over from me that day because the event could have been cancelled, but she was given the opportunity to find out what her capabilities were and she took it.

CHAPTER TWENTY-TWO

Some examples of how spirit works

I know that Spirit has given me healing whenever I have needed it, and therefore, given me a long life when it might have been otherwise. My mother had kidney problems and I have inherited a weakness in that area, but none of it concerns me because if I ask for healing, I get it. I am currently on six-weekly visits to the hospital for check-ups but everything still appears to be going well. My arthritis has not become too bad, despite the doctors telling me that I should expect to end up in a wheelchair. I also know that it is common for psychically sensitive people to have a traumatic experience in life that puts them on the path to working with Spirit, and that was the case with me.

Colleagues tend to agree with me that we do have some slight advance knowledge of our mediumistic tendencies. In my case it was the events that occurred when I was sixteen and the fact that my grandmother was psychic. Her explanations to me have proved subsequently to be a hundred per cent correct.

I believe that we are all born with these gifts to some extent, but choosing whether or not to develop them and use them is a purely personal matter. Some psychics who I know have worked in the field only because they were unable to avoid it. A clairaudient once told me that the voices he heard had persisted and persisted until he started working with them. Once he did so, things settled down, but that this was causing disruption in his life up until then.

I feel that, before we are born, we go into the "upstairs office" where a basic working plan for our time on earth is formulated, and that this becomes something that we have to follow. Call it destiny, fate or whatever. We then come down to earth and follow this plan, but if we choose deviate from the agreed path, Spirit will allow us that deviation and not force us back onto it. In my own experience, I have found that when I decided that I wanted to spend more time on myself rather than working with Spirit, my life would go around in a circle and then take me back to that decision point once again.

Giving up on life never worked for me. The seminal incident being when Olive intervened after I had made the decision to write some goodbye letters and turn the gas taps on. However, this was not the only time that I almost gave in to despair. After the abortive attempt to live and work in Grimsby, George Dale's son asked me to help him out and he borrowed some money from me to fix his car. Then George's wife had to go into a nursing home. Soon afterwards, my insurance company told me that they would longer cover me for taxi work due to my age, unless I was prepared to pay the full premium and not the discounted one. This amounted to £2,000 a year, which was something I could not afford. Once again, everything became totally overwhelming and I decided to end it all, despite the fact I was President of a Church at the time. I chose to do nothing for a while, but then I became ill, so I didn't even have the strength to go through with it.

*****

There was a very well known medium called David Young who performed stage demonstrations. He used to invite six members of the audience onto the stage and he commenced his demonstration by giving them all a reading, which meant that there was an entertainment value to his show as well as it being useful. One night in Worthing, a young man in his late thirties was invited onto the stage. David asked him if he had a girlfriend in the audience. He rather reluctantly confirmed that he had. David then said to him, " I have your wife here." (His wife being in Spirit).

The man said, rather worriedly, "Oh dear."

"No, it's not 'oh dear'," said David, "your wife she says she is pleased for you and she wants to ask why you haven't proposed to the lady in the audience."

The man was taken aback and said, "But my wife wouldn't like that."

"I'm sorry, but she says that she wants it and you're wrong in thinking that she wouldn't like it. She approves of the lady you are with now, so how about doing it here and now?"

After a bit more evidence being given to the man, he finally got down on one knee on the stage and he proposed to the lady in the audience.

She jumped up out of her seat, clapped her hands and cried, "Oh, yes!"

David asked the young man why he had not done it before and the man answered, "Well, I wanted to but I didn't feel that my wife would have approved."

"Well, you've received your answer tonight, haven't you? She does approve and - so does your mother!"

"My mother?" he asked.

"Oh yes, your mother is here as well."

The audience laughed at the sight of one very happy man walking off the stage that night!

*****

David Young always surprised me. He did a very good job not only because of what he did but also the way in which he worked. I often acted as master of ceremonies and I would stand at the side of the stage to make the introductions. I could see one poor medium smoking furiously before his show. Sometimes he had two cigarettes on the go at the same time! He was almost paralysed with nerves until he walked out on stage, but once he started speaking to the audience, he was fine.

David Young's events were always wonderful. He would give a demonstration and then take a break while another medium took over, then he would then come back onto the stage and finish the rest of the evening off. We began to notice that in coastal places such as Worthing, Bognor and so on, several of the same faces were appearing in the audience. We decided to set up a session during the interval where there was a "question and answer" exchange, and this was also hugely successful.

On another occasion, when we were working in Cardiff, one of our mediums assisted the Police with a murder enquiry. The Police visited the place where we were working and asked if any of us were prepared to sit and talk with them. I gather that the medium that they spoke with actually provided them with a lead to work on. The Police wrote to her afterwards to thank her, but the Police always work with Mediums in a "covert" way and they rarely admit that they use our expertise. This example shows that there are many avenues where a medium can help.

Editor's note: In my experience policemen, paramedics and so on accept what we do very easily, but they cannot use it as evidence in court.

*****

I have known a number of mediums who have not grown up with Spirit, but who have been mediumistic from a very young age. Some realised it when they were children or perhaps had parents who were psychic, while others needed to experience a special event to awaken them to Spirit. In my case, it was spine cancer and a friend who took me to a healer that started me off, but I have heard many similar stories from other people.

Some useful tips

If you find yourself getting interested in spiritual work, you should start to investigate it and also start to rely on your instincts. You should listen to advice from others, but always test this rather than swallowing it wholesale while you set yourself on the pathway to development.

I had one piece of good advice from Harry Edwards, one of my first teachers, at the start of my learning phase; this was:

"Take everything in, sift it, and keep what feels comfortable in your head. If you have any doubt, throw it out. Continue in that vein and then you will be working with the truth."

You must always believe that you can do it, but take advice, listen and always carry on learning. This is what I have been doing for the last forty years!

*****

For those of you who give readings or plan to do so, you should use a tape recorder because it will stop anyone disputing what you have said. People often edit what they hear, and from the time the words leave the reader's mouth to the time they reach the client's brain (let alone his memory), they can change out of all recognition. Sometimes a client will feel overwhelmed by the experience of having a reading or visiting a medium and they don't quite take in all that is being said to them. Some are foreign, so they need the tape in order to go back over it, to understand the English properly. Most, if not all, readers give their clients a recording of their reading. The client will think that it is for his or her benefit so that they don't have to scribble down notes, but it really is as much for the reader's benefit as well.

On more than one occasion, a client has phoned me after arriving home to say that their tape was blank. I would ask the client to bring it back to me if he or she lived nearby, or else to post it back. When I played the tape, I have always found that it played perfectly. When I questioned the client, I discovered that they had tried to play their tape to someone else. It seems that in some cases, Spirit didn't want the reading broadcast because it was personal to the person who had received it.

A good example of this occurred when I was living in Wallington. A lady came to see me and she appeared pleased with her reading. She took the tape and left. A couple of week's later, the lady's husband rang me. He gave me a heavy tirade about using poor quality tapes. This didn't make sense as I have always bought good quality tapes. He told me that the tape his wife had received had blank spaces on it and said that he was going to bring it back. I apologised to him but said he could not bring it back as the tape belonged to his wife and not to him. I told him that if he wanted a reading, he could come on his own and have one, but he could not return the tape - only his wife could. A few minutes later, his wife phoned and apologised for her husband. I told her it was all right, but that if there were blank spaces, she should bring it back to me and I would test it on my machine. She duly came to see me and brought the tape with her. I placed the tape into my machine and played it all the way through - there were no blank spaces! I was concentrating on the tape, but when the tape had finished, I noticed she was trying not to laugh - and then she laughed out loud. I asked her why she was laughing. She told me that the blank spaces that had been on the tape were things that Spirit had told her about her husband. I asked her if she had given her husband permission to listen to the tape. She said she had not; her husband had gone through her belongings, found the tape and had played it when she was not at home.

I said to her, "That's the answer. Those 'blanks' were obviously matters that related to him or that you have to talk to him about, and he was not meant to listen to them himself." I asked her if she understood.

She said, "Perfectly, in fact as soon as I played the tape at home, I knew straight away what had been in the blank spaces."

I suggested that she should listen to the tape in private, then explain to her husband why the blank spaces had occurred. Spirit does work in unusual ways with us at times. If I should ever have a dud tape, I would invite the client back and give them another reading.

I feel that Spirit looks after us when we are working. Even after we have finished our job, Spirit remains on guard so that anybody who is not supposed to hear what has been said cannot hear it - and in that way, they are unable to do anything about it. Spirit will always work with the truth and will not assist anyone who attempts to work without it.

CHAPTER TWENTY-THREE

Of motorcycles and mechanical objects

You may remember the story about how a strange vehicle gave me a lift to the military camp when I was in the Navy. Here is another tale that is similar in nature.

I was on my way out from a festival in the Midlands, feeling very tired after having completed a day's work. A religious sect which was busily demonstrating against what we had been doing besieged my colleagues and me. On this particular occasion, I found myself being berated by a rather aggressive man who said that he was going to "teach me a lesson". Out of the blue, somebody grabbed his arm and the man swung around to find out who had touched him. While this was going on, I took the opportunity to walk away, but when I looked back to thank the man who had grabbed his arm - there was no one there! I walked away thinking about this and realised that sometimes we receive help in a really significant manner, while at other times the help isn't this obvious.

*****

While living in Grimsby, I became secretary of the Cleethorpes Church, and then I was voted in as President. However, before accepting this post, I made a point of telling the members about a number of things that they may not have approved of. I told them that I belonged to BAPS, and that I used my gifts in various ways. I told them that I gave readings at festivals but that I used the cards for this purpose, because it was not possible to fully open spiritually when a crowd of two thousand people was wandering around. I also told them that I used the Runes and even on occasion a crystal ball, and in addition to all these sins, I had also trained to be a white witch at some point in the past. I said that if they still wanted me that I would be happy to accept the position of President. There was silence for a few seconds until an elderly man stood up. I only knew him as "Old Bob" and he was a great heckler who always had something to say. I expected him to oppose me after my revelations, but instead he said, "Friends, I don't know what you feel, but if a man can stand up and admit to the truth, then I want him as President." There was a huge round of applause. So that was how I became the President of Cleethorpes Church.

Numerous events took place in the church during the week. We had two healing nights and an open Circle night where anyone could come in and chat. Another night was dedicated to a closed Circle, and this was run by another medium. I sometimes popped into the open Circle, but only by invitation to the closed Circle. We took in turns controlling the service on a rota basis. Sunday was a normal service day.

I recall one occasion when it was my turn to be in charge. It was a Saturday evening and a clairvoyant night. I opened up the Church and went into the kitchen to put the urn on to boil so that we could have tea and coffee later. I went to the platform to tidy up and then waited for the others to arrive. The Church was almost full, as the medium who was expected was quite a popular one in the area. I waited but nobody else turned up. Nobody came! None of my team arrived. Not the usher or the tea and coffee makers - and more importantly, no medium! The time arrived when I had no choice but to commence the service and had to say to the congregation that I was very sorry but it looked like I was the only one there.

"Old Bob" was there, and he said, "Right Gordon, then you'd better get on and do it."

"No Bob, I'm getting a 'no' from Spirit, but we'll do the healing and have the normal opening prayers and hymns.

Fortunately, the pianist had turned up and she had chosen the selection of hymns for the congregation to sing that evening.

We sang the opening hymn, said the prayers, together with the healing prayers then sang the "interval hymn", as I used to call it. After that, there should have been the clairvoyance demonstration. I stood up and said that we could either have a "question and answer session" or that everyone could go home; according to whatever the congregation preferred to do. There was a momentary silence. I broke it by saying that I wanted to put a question to the congregation. My question was that I had always been curious about those people who haven't grown up with the knowledge of Spirit, but who had then come into it to work as mediums or healers, so I asked the congregation how they became interested. Some answered my question, and this led on to a stream of questions and answers which carried on until our normal time for closing down. Near the end, a man put his hand up and said he would like to ask a question. He said, "I want to know what your opinion is as to what happens to those who commit suicide."

I replied, "If people commit suicide for unselfish reasons, they are allowed to enter the Spirit realm, but they have to return some time later to complete their time here on earth. If, however, it was for selfish reasons, then they go into a "limbo" state until it's their normal time to return and do not enter into the Spirit realm.

While speaking to him I suddenly heard the sound of a Harley Davidson 1000 c.c. motorcycle. I knew the sound very well because my father used to have one. While they are very powerful machines and comfortable to ride (so my father used to tell me) I could never ride a motorbike, and it was not until I started working for Spirit that I found out why. Apparently, when I was being carried in my mother's womb, my mother was riding pillion with my father when they had a motorcycle accident. After that incident, she never got back on a motorcycle again. Spirit and doctors have told me that her fear had transmitted itself to me. I only ever rode a motorcycle once, under duress - and I was absolutely terrified!

The rider of the motorcycle that I was hearing clairaudiently kept revving his machine, but in between the revs I could hear a voice saying, "I am okay and I am on Spiritual community service." Then the sound of the motorcycle disappeared.

I asked the man who had spoken whether his brother ever had a 1000 c.c. Harley Davidson motorcycle. He confirmed that he had and told me that he had absolutely idolised it. I said, "Well, he's just been here and he's told me to tell you that he's okay and that he's on Spiritual community service. I am also getting an indication from my "friend" that this is correct, because I did not catch all the words from your brother, other than that he said that he would be in touch." The man in the congregation was crying, but he thanked me and said that he had never received a message from his brother before. You can see that Spirit sometimes has peculiar ways of getting things across to us.

I continued answering the questions for another hour and twenty minutes! Then I drew the evening to a close saying, "Well my friends, I'm going to stop now. Is there anyone who will volunteer to go into the kitchen to make the refreshments for us? The urn is on."

Two ladies from the back of the Church immediately offered to make the refreshments and one or two others promptly offered to help me tidy up. The questions and answers were still continuing when I walked in to join them.

*****

Not long after that particular evening, another Annual General Meeting was held. I had been President for two years, but this time another member was voted in as President. I thought there must be a reason for the decision, but it was two or three months later before it became apparent that it was when I had to move back to the outer London area!

I still attend the larger festivals such as the Mind, Body and Spirit Festivals at Victoria, Alexandra Palace and Manchester. I still teach at Pat Dickie's hotel seminars in Bournemouth at the end of October or the beginning of November every year. I still do postal readings using the cards and I also give readings from hand-written letters, as I am able to tune in on the "vibrations" of the handwriting.

Even now, there are occasions when I feel that I am being tested. An example happened to me three years ago when I was in Manchester at the Mind, Body and Spirit Festival. The drill is that the receptionist on the stand hands a ticket to the client, which is marked with the name of the reader that the client has chosen to see. The assistant to the receptionist on this particular day was a young boy called Colin. He came to my table, took my client's chair away and then gave me the client's ticket. I asked him what was going on.

All he would say was, "You'll see."

I looked along the gangway and saw an electric wheelchair that was being operated by mouth carrying a lady who was coming to see me. She positioned her wheelchair opposite me. I looked at the lady and saw she had a nice face but her arms were no longer than six or seven inches in length, and her legs were only a little longer. Basically, I was faced with a torso perched on the wheelchair. I asked the lady if it was possible for her to shuffle the cards and she confirmed that she could. She did too - and quite dextrously - and then she handed the cards back to me.

I laid the cards out and I couldn't believe what my "friend" was telling me to say, as none of it made sense for someone in her position. Somewhat unwillingly I said what I was being told to say and then just worked through the rest of the reading. When I finished, I was feeling a little bit weary, but when I looked at the lady I saw that she had a big smile on her face. She thanked me and I asked her if she had understood the reading. She replied, "Yes, perfectly. You've answered all the questions I had in my head and you've also given me some advice as to what to do with my children and my husband."

She saw my expression and said, "Yes, I'm married and I have two children, and what's more, I do what you're doing at the home where I live, but I wanted to know if I'm still doing it right, and you've told me that I am."

I thanked her for letting me know and handed her the tape, which she put into the bag hanging off of her chest. With that, she turned the wheelchair around and away she went.

I sat back and mentally said, "Thank you Spirit, for being with me, but you certainly gave me a test of faith!" All I received back was a chuckle.

We are occasionally "put under the hammer" by Spirit as a test of our faith.

*****

Spirit has a sense of humour

One day I had a laughable experience. Many people seem to think that Spirit is always serious, but this is not the case. While I was at the investigation stage of my journeys, I attended a service in Clapham to see a well-known medium who was demonstrating "direct voice" to restricted numbers at his house. When I arrived, the secretary asked me for seventeen shillings and six pence in old money for my entrance fee. I only had a pound on me at the time, so I handed it over. The lady had run out of change, so she said that she would tell the medium and that they would give me my change later. I thoroughly enjoyed the evening and found the whole experience exhilarating, and I went home. I had completely forgotten about the two shillings and six pence that they still owed me.

Many years later, I was acting as the Chairman to a medium. As he came on to the platform he said to me, "Before we start, Gordon, I have a message for you. I have someone here who wants to give you the two shillings and six pence that they owe you, and they are sorry that they did not give it to you before they passed. They will keep it until you join them." I suddenly remembered back to the event that the medium was talking about.

I relayed this story to the congregation, and as you can imagine, this caused quite a lot of laughter in the Church.

*****

People sometimes ask me whether or not Spirit is able to operate mechanical or electrical objects. I think the following story may answer that one. One of the members in my Circle was called Rodney Peacock. He was one of my pupils at one time but he is now working as a medium. One evening, we had a discussion about whether Spirit was able to operate mechanical and electrical objects. Rodney was adamant that this was impossible and Spirit is incapable of such things. We were debating this for quite some time and I began to lose patience with him, but he persisted with his protestations saying that Spirit would never be so frivolous. This turned out to be one of those occasions when I wished I had had a camera in my hand because only a few moments later, Rodney nearly jumped out of his skin - he certainly jumped off of his chair and ran over to the other side of the room!

During the debate, Rodney had been sitting alongside a mantelpiece in my flat. Sitting on the mantelpiece was a musical cigarette lighter that belonged to a friend who had asked me to repair it, as it was supposed to play a tune when it was operated. I had taken the movement out of the casing, so the "works" were nowhere near the switch that operated it. The lighter was just lying there in pieces when it suddenly started to play a tune. The only person near it was Rodney, so when it started playing it was right by his ear! At first, Rodney accused me of having controlled it somehow from where I was sitting. Up to that point, Rodney had been strongly opinionated and accustomed to thinking that he knew all the answers and was never wrong. The change in Rodney meant that the atmosphere of the Circle improved from then on, so not only did Spirit bring laughter to the Circle, but it also proved that the Spirits can find ingenious ways of getting their message across.

*****

You should learn to rely on your own instincts and to trust and work with what you feel in your heart. Spirit is always looking after us. Here is another example of this.

One Monday, I had felt a strong urge to visit my friend, Peter. I knew that Mondays were awkward, as he would be preparing for the following evening's show. I decided to ignore my feelings and spend the day as I had first intended - anyway I was due to visit Peter later in the week. On the Wednesday morning another friend phoned me to tell me that Peter had gone to bed Tuesday evening but had not woken up... he had passed over.

That taught me that such strong impulses should not be ignored, regardless of any material obstacles that might be in the way, and that I must follow up on them. Only then would I be doing what Spirit wanted me to do, so from that day on, I have paid attention to such feelings. Spirit teaches us to do what we should do and to keep our promises.

*****

Spirit gives us awareness that can come in many forms. Here is an example.

In 2001, I spent Christmas in Holland with a very good friend of mine called Léni. One morning, while I was eating breakfast, Léni asked me whether the name Gregory meant anything to me.

"Yes," I replied, "it most certainly does. Why?"

Léni said, "Well, I have a gentleman here by that name and he tells me that he was an Abbot at Glastonbury. He is dressed in a black hooded robe, tied with a white rope-like belt. He has a square-cut beard and he is laughing. How do you know of him?"

I explained to Léni that this was the same monk who had appeared to Ollie way back at the time that I was contemplating suicide. I had since found out that he was at Glastonbury at around 600 AD, and I also discovered that I had been at Glastonbury abbey with him in a previous incarnation. I had found this out while visiting Glastonbury and when I had gone for a walk on my own. I stood under a tree looking across the ruined Abbey when time seemed to slip back, and I suddenly "saw" everything as it had been in 600 A.D. I saw the monks going about their business and I could also see people working in the fields near the abbey.

Léni was astounded. We had always said that from the moment we first met, we felt as though we had always known each other, but we could not understand why. Apparently Leni had also been around in Glastonbury at that time, so at last we made the link. An amazing coincidence, maybe, but Gregory was obviously aware of this and proved that he is still with us.

*****

A man with whom I worked briefly when I was in the early stages of learning, used to say, "Whenever you teach or talk about Spirit - keep it simple." When someone asked him why this was, he would answer, "Because even the village idiot needs to be able understand you. I am not being derogatory to anybody, but Spiritual understanding is best kept simple so that everybody can understand it. It is easier to assimilate if it is simple."

Remember to always work with truth and simplicity.

For those of you who read this book, please remember that when you work with Spirit, it is part of your life. It is not just a separate compartment that you keep to one side. It is similar to being deeply involved in an orthodox religion, being something that becomes part of your life. I do not mean that Spirit is involved at every moment of your life, but it certainly kicks in when you are faced with important decisions.

Spirit becomes part of your life because you want to make the world a better place and to try and spread peace around by your thoughts and actions. I have never set out to hurt anyone - and this is even more the case since I have acknowledged Spirit. I have not always succeeded in this, but I have always tried to bear this in mind through the years.

CHAPTER TWENTY-FOUR

Summary

Are we born with this gift or do we choose to learn it?

A healer, medium, clairvoyant, psychic or whatever you wish to call us, we will have agreed prior to being born to use these gifts at some time in our lives.

Looking back, I now know that I should have started using my abilities long before I did so. I realise that for too many years, I had been too concerned with making money and getting on in life. Perhaps I had to be. When Joyce and I moved into a brand new house in Crawley in the 1950s we had little furniture, but in the matter of a month or so, our house was furnished. Joyce had borrowed £3,500, which was a vast sum of money in those days. I had to work at a day job and also at other jobs in the evenings and at weekends in order to pay off these debts. I did not have the time then to study to discover what Spirit was about. Having said that, just as teachers are better for doing some other work between leaving college and taking up their career, it is probably necessary for us to live ordinary lives and to experience ordinary pains, disappointments and problems before taking up this work.

I guess that my first experience of the "other side" was when I played with Spirit children around the old oak tree, but that is a common childhood event, even among people who "forget" the spiritual side of life and never have any more to do with it.

My first memorable happening was when I saw and heard my late aunt during the night of heavy bombing when I was sixteen. Again, this is not an unusual experience, although most people find such an occurrence unnerving.

The next was the one related to my father and his trip back after death to prove that his soul had indeed survived. This was linked to the death of my brother, and the fact that I saw him going over, when others who were in the room did not.

The real turning point was the awful time when I fell ill with spinal cancer and Joyce left me, taking the children with her. The visits to the healer at this time led directly to me becoming a healer myself.

When a message comes your way, it is as well to take it on board and keep it at the back of your mind. When the same message arises again, you may still keep it on ice, but you will know for certain that it was meant. Either then or after a third reminder, you should start to work with it. This is how I came to write this book.

A medium gave me the message that I should write this memoir. Although I acknowledged the fact, I put it to the back of my mind because it was not something that I had ever actually considered, but a second prompting came a few months later. I was attending the Mind, Body and Spirit Festival in London when a client came for a reading. This client was a medium who I knew but on this occasion she chose to consult me because she had a few problems in her life. When I finished reading for her, I asked her if she had any questions she wanted to put to me. She said she didn't, but she then told me that she had a message to give me. She said, "They're asking 'what about the book?'"

The subject arose for the third time in October 2000, when I spent a week teaching at Pat Dickie's psychic seminar in Bournemouth. During a break, I got into conversation with a lady called Jacqueline Towers who was attending the event as a student. During this conversation, the idea of my writing a book came up again. I began to look at the suggestion more seriously, but I considered the prospect to be impossible, because my arthritis means that I can no longer hold a pen for more than a few moments at a time. While I can still type, I can't keep it up for very long.

A few weeks later Jackie rang me to ask for my help. It turned out that she had taken a job that involved audio typing and she wanted some work to practice on at home. I asked her what I could do to help and she suggested that I start to put my story on tape for her to type up - just for the practice, of course. I told her that I had thought about writing my story but hadn't really put my mind to it. Jackie is also a psychic, so when she said, "Don't think about it - just do it!" I took notice.

I dictated one tape and listened to it - thinking that it was rubbish, I started again. When I was satisfied with what I had produced I sent off the first tape. I continued dictating my tapes and sending them off. Jackie typed from the tapes and (amazingly) she also thanked me for the opportunity I had given for her to practice. Whilst she was working from my tapes Jackie started to have a few strange encounters and events herself, and she also told me how much she was learning from the information on the tapes.

*****

I feel that everyone should have an open mind and maintain his or her own beliefs but never condemn anyone else for theirs. The one thing that I am very serious about is that God gave us the gift of free will and freedom of choice, and we are fortunate enough to live in the wealthy western world where we can exercise that gift. I wish this was a worldwide situation, but that is not the case.

Please always remember that free will and freedom of choice is right, and people must be allowed to have it. It is no good telling someone that they must do something if it is against their nature or their desires. You must respect their wishes and work with them rather than against them.

I am still teaching and still seeing the occasional individual. I am old now and I realise that I am getting close to the point where I will "go home" and discover whether what I have done in this life has been as it should be. I am ready to answer for the things I have neglected to do. I do regret that I have not worked as much with Spirit as I could have done.

The real regret that I have is that I do not know my children at all. My son, Philip Glynn Wyndham was born on 29 December 1948 at Central Middlesex Hospital in Park Royal. My twin daughters, Karen Elizabeth and Andrea Jayne were born on 25 September 1957 at Redhill County Hospital. Due to circumstances beyond my control, I haven't seen them since the time when Philip was sixteen and Karen and Andrea were nine. I have often wondered if they have discovered or used the gift that they inherited from me. Not a day goes by without them being in my thoughts, and I often wonder if Spirit will allow me to meet them before I pass over myself. It is the only wish that I have left.

Take care, everyone, and God bless. I wish you well in your learning.

Editor's note: As we know, within a few days of writing this final passage of his wonderful book, Gordon Arthur Smith finally passed over.

God bless you Gordon, from your friends, Jackie Towers and Sasha Fenton.

POST SCRIPT

Editor's note: *After Gordon's death, Jackie and I received several letters from his friends and we decided to reproduce them here. Some are serious, some are sad and others are a celebration of the fun and humour shared between Gordon and his many friends. I have not edited these letters, they are just as the people wrote them. The somewhat strangled English in Leni's letter reflects the fact that Leni is Dutch, but the love that she expresses shines brightly through.*

From Rashid

In the words of Puff Daddy...

"You gave me the strength I need to proceed.
You gave me the strength I need to believe.
Till the day we meet again,
In my heart is where I keep you, friend."

May god bless you on your journey into the light and beyond the veil.

All my love,

Rashid Ahmad, London, July 2002

*****

From Léni

Meeting Mr Gordon Smith

I learned about him over the phone by long talks with a female friend that I found in the Arthur Findlay College.

In those days she turned to him for advice whenever she was struggling with something. So, I wanted to know whom she was confiding in and if he was to my standards. This sounds awful, but I can be very protective where friends are concerned, especially when they themselves are not well balanced. I had good feeling, though. When we entered his house he greeted Tony first, looked at me and said: "Oh well" and gave me a hug. This is not normal for me, Gordon said very surprised. Nevertheless, I replied that he knew who was coming before I even was in England, and he grinned. But there was a mutual feeling of knowing one another.

Before we went away after a visit that stretched from 10.30 until almost 18.00 hours, he said that he would visit me in Holland. Afterwards he phoned me and said that Tony was coming and that he would accompany her if that were all right. But I said no, friend, you are coming and Tony is accompanying you so you won't get lost. But I am so ashamed, he said, I imposed myself on you, but it is your own fault. You made me puzzle how the hell you were and what you were doing to me. Making me do things that I never would or dared to do!

Well, we found out during the few visits he made to Holland that our friendship dates back at least to the early days of Glastonbury. There were so many deep spiritual conversations, so much to share about our lives and so much teasing and joking.

I feel honoured that I was allowed to meet him, overjoyed that at least I had him last year for a fortnight during Christmas and New Year. Anyway when you meet someone so very sweet, gentleman like, knowledgeable, spiritual and a real, real friend, it is always too late. And when you have to let them go, it is always too early. And it hurts, although I know that he was more than prepared to go. It is a bit double, sadness on one hand and joy for him at the other.

On behalf of all my family members and all my friends here in Holland that met him and loved him right away, I want to say: "Dear friend, none of us will ever forget you!"

Léni Hooijshuur, Zaandam, Holland, July 2002

*****

From Lorraine

I was terribly upset to hear of Gordon's death, even though I knew it to be imminent. I spoke to him a couple of weeks ago, and he was giving me an update on the book. I "knew" without him having to tell me, that he was only waiting to complete the book, before joining his mates "upstairs". So, when Sheila rang me last week to tell me, I wasn't surprised, just terribly, terribly saddened. For myself I may add, not for him.

He has been my friend and mentor for more years that I care to remember, and even though months would pass without contact, he always knew when I needed him. Sure enough, when the going would get tough, or my continuous ill health would really get me down, the phone would ring, and it would be Gordon. I can remember wailing down the phone to him on one occasion, moaning about how much pain I was in, and how I must have done something truly dreadful at some stage, to be "punished" so. How on earth did he cope with the terrible problems he had, particularly with his poor health? He laughed, and in that soft gentle way of his, told me that he looked on his life as a blessing, and that if he had been born with a silver spoon in his mouth and with excellent health, he would never have been able to develop the love, humility, empathy and deep, deep appreciation of others suffering, and never having experienced it, how would he be able to help them? One of the many lessons I learnt from Gordon was how to turn self-pity into a positive force.

It was Gordon who guided my first faltering steps along my Spiritual path, and who showed me that it was OK that my path wasn't necessarily that of others. It was Gordon who first pushed me into the role of Tutor when I didn't think I was good enough. It was Gordon that would make sense of the world when I couldn't. He taught me so many things, and helped me become a much better person than I ever thought I could be. He never lost patience with me, disapproved, scolded or reprimanded me, even when I'm sure I deserved it, and he never ever lost faith in me. What he taught me by example, kindness and love. I shall miss him desperately, but I know that if there is any way possible, Gordon will contact me, just to let me know he is OK, and that he will be there for me as he has always been. Knowing Gordon, I have no doubt that he will keep his promise. Rest well my friend, you deserve it.

Lorraine Hall, Cornwall, July 2002

*****

From Marlene

Gordon was a man of considerable intelligence and charm, but it was his spirituality that left a lasting impression.

Marlene Houghton, London, July 2002

*****

From Shileen

Dear Gordon,

Well, I finally sent the last photograph of you to Sasha for your book. I knew it would have been the last photo, and you knew also, because your friends from Spirit were talking to you to start another spirit and mind festival. You will never retire because BAPS and the spiritual work will continue. Say hello to Barbara Cracknell, Renee Hindle, David Young and Peter Bridges for me.

Yes, we will all miss you, my Peacepipe, Sir Gordon Smith. You were like that old faithful armchair, always there when we needed you. Nothing was too much trouble, always on time whenever I travelled with you to countless psychic fairs over many years. Telling the same stories, I would doze for a few minutes, "did you year what I just said?" "Yes, Gordon, I remembered that story!" Especially when we couldn't get out the car park because the attendant wanted more money, but I knew you had already paid the man - life was never boring. You helped so many people, not only did the clients get a reading but your mates showed them their own way home.

You made me laugh, Peacepipe. You voted to be President last year. I said that you could have my hat any time. Well, you said you had been everything else in the committee except president. Well, Peacepipe, not only have you many, many hats now, but also wings to fly, but not sure about the halo!!

All those that had the privilege of having met Sir Gordon Smith will know what I mean by there will never be another Wizard of the World like him. He will be very much missed by his family with BAPS. Here comes his pipe smoke again. Enjoy your new life. We love you.

Your dear friend,
Shileen Rogers, Clacton, July 2002

*****

From Astrid

I first met Gordon approximately six years ago. At that time, I had just lost my father and Gordon became a "father" substitute to me. Over the years, I leaned on him and he was always there for me, both on a personal level as well as with the encouragement and advice he gave me in connection with my own healing work. He was a wonderful spiritual teacher to me. He was such a good listener, always helpful, loving and giving of himself. What I liked about him most was his total commitment to his spirituality, which showed through in the way he dealt with people. He was always kind and offered encouragement to others rather than condemnation. I had enormous respect for him and his work.

It was Gordon who introduced me to the Surrey Healing Association as well as the Psychic Seminars held in Bournemouth each year, both of which progressed me along my own path of being able to heal others.

Gordon, I will always remember you with love and you will be greatly missed. You are an enormous loss to me.

With thanks and respect,
Astrid Hensen, London, July 2002

172

British Astrological and Psychic Society (BAPS)

Gordon Arthur Smith joined BAPS many years ago, and was an active member for the rest of his life.

The qualifications earned through their study courses and the benefits of membership are valuable assets if you are interested in studying for a recognized qualification in practically any divination, either as a part- or full-time Reader.

BAPS and Zambezi Publishing come together in developing reading matter and standard texts for many of their courses, and many of our books are available from BAPS; at a special discount if you are a BAPS member, and in some cases, books are supplied as part of the course material.

If you wish to contact BAPS for further information, their address details are given below.

~~~~~

These are a selection of the courses available from BAPS, some of which are already accompanied by Zambezi Publishing text books:
Psychic perception ~ Astrology ~ Classical Astrology ~ Karmic Astrology ~ Tarot ~ Palmistry ~ Chinese Oracles & Feng Shui ~ Crystal Divination ~ Dream Interpretation ~ Graphology ~ Numerology ~ Practical Witchcraft & Magic ~ Introduction to Alternative Health.

~~~~~

Please address enquiries to:
Department Z
British Astrological and Psychic Society
P.O. Box 363
ROCHESTER ME1 3DH

~~~~~

Tel: +44 (0)906 479 9827
Fax: +44 (0)1634 323 006
web: www.baps.ws   email: info@baps.ws

Prophecy for Profit

"The Essential Career & Business Guide for those who give Readings"

Sasha Fenton & Jan Budkowski

The right price for consultations...   Startup costs...

The equipment you need...   Building up your clientele...

Finances & cashflow...   Organisational methods...

Your spiritual pathway...   Psychic protection...

The Media...   Stress and the

self-employed...

The Marine Bandsman Syndrome...   A mental & physical health

guide...

and teaching & lecturing...

~~~~~

Internationally recognized Astrologer, Tarot Reader, Palmist, Psychic and Author with sales of over 6 million books; who else but Sasha could produce a guide like this one?

Together with her husband Jan Budkowski, who adds over thirty years of financial and banking expertise, their combination delivers the most authoritative – yet easily readable – work of this nature that any consultant could ask for.

~~~~~

If you're serious about your career, you need this book!

ISBN 0-9533478-1-8   £10.95
240 pages

Reading the Runes
"A Beginner's Guide"
Kim Farnell

Kim's book is the official text for the BAPS Rune Reading course. It covers the history, mythology and meaning behind each Rune, for the purpose of divination. Kim offers advice for making and energising your Runes and she suggests numerous traditional Rune spreads to suit a variety of purposes.

~~~~~

Kim gives a thorough explanation and interpretation for each Rune, both in its upright and reversed positions.

~~~~~

Here, you will even find explanations of how each Rune can be used for magic and meditation.

~~~~~

This is an all-round manual for those who want to read the Runes for personal guidance, or even as part of a professional consultant's package of divinatory skills.

~~~~~

ISBN 1-903065-26-7   £8.99
176 pages

Star*Date*Oracle
"Ancient Lore for Today's World"
Sasha Fenton & Jonathan Dee

Got a problem?
Need a quick decision?
Choose the right day for:
~ Getting a job
~ That hot date
~ Travel & holiday planning
Fixing things at home,
or planning anything else...

The Star*Date*Oracle highlights your best timing,
for any hour, any day, any year!
~~~~~

Also included:-
The LIST OF FATES reveals the destiny
in the name you use every day –
not necessarily your birthname or an unloved "official" name.

The **MYSTIC PYRAMID** unleashes your own intuition,
helped by your Guardian Angel, and gives instant answers to your
problems.
*The sources are ancient, but the system and results are
right up-to-date, easy to understand and to use!*

ISBN 1-903065-15-1   £5.99
192 pages

Fortune Telling by Tarot Cards
"A Beginner's Guide to Understanding the Tarot"
Sasha Fenton

Sasha brings over a quarter of a century of experience with the Tarot into this comprehensive Teach-Yourself Tarot book, taking the subject all the way through from a beginner's standpoint to a professional level.

Added to the usual Tarot book material, this new, revised edition of Sasha's 500,000 copy topselling guide contains valuable information and considerations arising from Tarot students' questions - in particular, how to overcome the problem of linking apparently conflicting cards to make a lucid, synthesized reading.

~~~~~

Contents include:-

Interpreting the cards - why readings don't always work - spreads & their uses - how to link cards easily - what happened after the guinea-pig readings in the previous edition!

~~~~~

Striking new Tarot card illustrations throughout, designed by the acknowledged historian and astrologer, Jonathan Dee!

ISBN 1-903065-18-6   £9.99

208 pages

Zambezi Publishing
"Much more than just books..."

All our books are available from good bookshops throughout the UK; many are available in the USA, sometimes under different titles and ISBNs used by our USA co-publisher, Sterling Publishing Co, Inc.

Please note:-
Nowadays, no bookshop can hope to carry in stock more than a fraction of the books produced each year (over 130,000 new titles were released in the Uk last year!). However, most UK bookshops can easily order and supply our titles within a matter of days.
Alternatively, you can find all our books on www.amazon.co.uk.

~~~~~

If you have any difficulty in sourcing one of our titles, then contact us at:-
Zambezi Publishing
P.O. Box 221, Plymouth
Devon PL2 2EQ
UK
Fax: +44 (0)1752 350 453

or on the Internet at:
web: www.zampub.com   email: info@zampub.com

(Want to join our mail list? It is NOT shared with anyone else, and is very sporadic – just email us your details, specifying snailmail or email preference).

If you enjoyed this book,
have a look at some of these, and on the previous pages:-

Family Sun Signs
How you Blend or Conflict
with your Loved Ones

The Hidden Zodiac
Why you differ from others
with your Sun Sign

Your Secret Moon
Moon Signs, Nodes & Occultations

Fortune Teller's Handbook
A fun way to discover your future

Super Tarot
How to link the cards to tell the Future...

Astrology... on the Move!
Where on Earth should you be...?

Tea Cup Reading
Tasseography - the ancient art of
reading Tea Leaves & Coffee Grounds

The Money Book
A Layman's Guide for Uncertain Times
(Available: July 2003)

How to be Psychic
A practical Guide to
Psychic Development
(Available: September 2003)

An Astrological Apothecary
The Astrology of Health,
Well-being & Stress Management
(Available: September 2003)

Tarot Mysteries
Origins, Symbolism & Meanings
of the Tarot Cards
(Available: September 2003)

Modern Palmistry
A Unique Guide to Hand Analysis
(Available: September 2003)